FULL STEAM AHEAD

For the Railways of Wales and the West Country 2010-2011

EDITOR
John Robinson

First Edition

ACKNOWLEDGEMENTS

We were greatly impressed by the friendly and cooperative manner of the staff and helpers of the railways and societies which we selected to appear in this book, and wish to thank them all for the help they have given. In addition we wish to thank Bob Budd (cover design) and Michael Robinson (page layouts) for their help. Also Lionel Parker and members of the Frimley and Ascot Locomotive Club for providing two of the photographs used on the cover.

We are particularly indebted to Peter Bryant for his invaluable assistance. Peter's web site: www.miniaturerailwayworld.co.uk provides a great deal of information about Miniature Railways in the UK.

Although we believe that the information contained in this guide is accurate at the time of going to press, we, and the Railways and Societies itemised, are unable to accept liability for any loss, damage, distress or injury suffered as a result of any inaccuracies. Furthermore, we and the Societies are unable to guarantee operating and opening times which may always be subject to cancellation without notice.

John Robinson

EDITOR

British Library Cataloguing in Publication Data

A catalogue record for this book is available from the British Library

ISBN-13:   978-1-86223-194-8

Copyright © 2010, MARKSMAN PUBLICATIONS. (01472 696226)
72 St. Peter's Avenue, Cleethorpes, N.E. Lincolnshire, DN35 8HU, England

Printed in the UK by The Cromwell Press Group

FOREWORD

The aim of this series of guides is to showcase the great range of UK railways, large and small. In deciding areas covered by this guide we have tried to stick to county boundaries wherever possible but, in a few cases, railways located close to the borders between counties may appear in both this and other guides in the series!

Although they are not strictly railways, we have included both the Great Orme and the Seaton Tramways as they have rails and are really great places to visit!

Copies of the seven railway guides which are shown on the rear cover of this book can be purchased UK post free from:

Marksman Publications
72 St. Peter's Avenue
Cleethorpes
N.E. Lincolnshire
DN35 8HU

Alternatively, these books can be ordered via our web site: www.stillsteaming.com

COVER PHOTOGRAPHS

From Standard gauge right down to 7¼ inch gauge, our cover photographs show the Bodmin & Wenford Railway, the Fairbourne Railway and the Conwy Valley Railway Museum respectively.

We are grateful to the Fairbourne Railway for supplying their photo and giving permission for it's use.

RAILWAY LOCATOR MAP

The numbers shown on this map relate to the page numbers for each railway.
Pages 8-10 contain an alphabetical listing of the railways featured in this guide.
Please note that the markers on this map show the approximate location only.

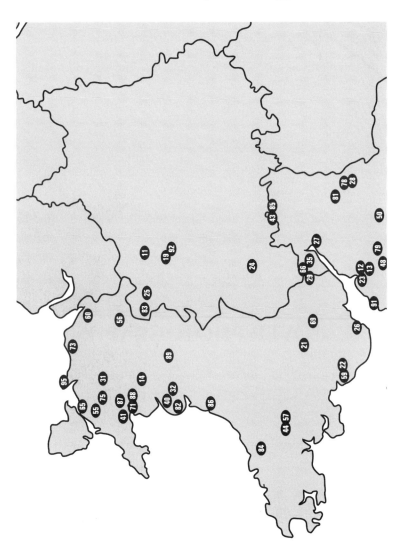

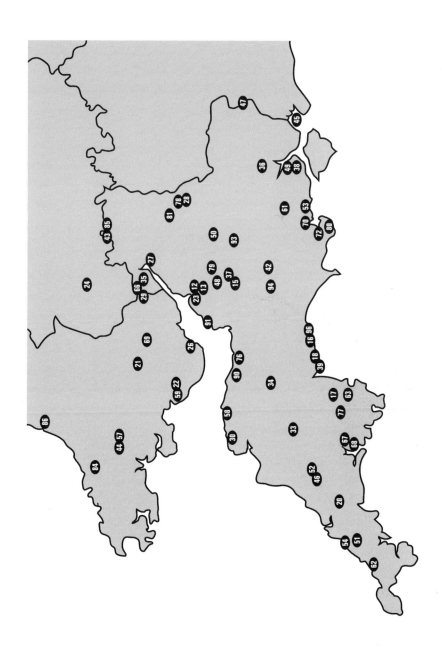

CONTENTS

ALDERNEY RAILWAY

Address: P.O. Box 75, Alderney, Channel Islands GY9 3DA	**Nº of Steam Locos**: None at present
Telephone Nº: None	**Nº of Other Locos**: 2
Year Formed: 1978	**Nº of Members**: 50
Location of Line: Braye Harbour to Mannez Quarry, Alderney	**Annual Membership Fee**: £15.00
	Approx Nº of Visitors P.A.: 2,000+
	Gauge: Standard
Length of Line: 2 miles	**Web site**: www.alderneyrailway.com

Photo courtesy of David Staines

GENERAL INFORMATION

Nearest Mainline Station: Not applicable
Nearest Bus Station: Not applicable
Car Parking: Available on site
Coach Parking: Available on site
Souvenir Shop(s): Yes
Food & Drinks: None at the Railway itself but available nearby

SPECIAL INFORMATION

The original line was built during the 1840s to assist in the construction of the large breakwater in Braye Harbour and fortifications on the island.
The line itself opened in 1847 and was the first nationalised railway run by the Admiralty.

OPERATING INFORMATION

Opening Times: Weekends and Bank Holidays from Easter until the September with a Santa Special also running in December. Trains usually run at 2.30pm and 3.30pm but also at 4.00pm during July and August.
Steam Working: None at present
Prices: Adult Return £4.50
 Child Return £3.00

Detailed Directions:
The Railway is situated adjacent to Braye Harbour.

ASHTON COURT ESTATE MINIATURE RAILWAY

Address: Ashton Court Estate, Long Ashton, North Somerset BS8 3PX	**Nº of Steam Locos**: 2
Telephone Nº: (0117) 963-9174	**Nº of Other Locos**: 3
Year Formed: Opened 1973	**Nº of Members**: 250
Location of Line: Ashton Court Estate	**Approx Nº of Visitors P.A.**: 30,000
Length of Line: Two tracks, each approximately a third of a mile in length	**Gauge**: 3½ inches, 5 inches & 7¼ inches
	Web site: www.bristolmodelengineers.co.uk

GENERAL INFORMATION

Nearest Mainline Station: Bristol Temple Meads (Approximately 5 miles)
Nearest Bus Station: Bristol (4 miles)
Car Parking: Free parking available on site
Coach Parking: Available by prior arrangement
Souvenir Shop(s): None
Food & Drinks: None

SPECIAL INFORMATION

The Railway is owned and operated by the Bristol Society of Model & Experimental Engineers which was founded in 1909.

OPERATING INFORMATION

Opening Times: Bank Holidays and some Sundays between April and mid-October (22 public passenger carrying days per year). Please contact the railway for a list of dates. On operating days, trains run from 12.00pm to 5.15pm.
Steam Working: All operating days.
Prices: 60p per ride per person. Ticket discounts for multiple rides are available.

Detailed Directions by Car:
Exit the M5 at junction 19 and take the A369 towards Bristol. After approximately 6 miles, just past the B3129 traffic lights is Ashton Court Estate. However, there is no right turn from this direction. Instead, take the side road on the left (North Road), turn right into Bridge Road and continue straight across the A369 at the traffic lights into the Clifton Lodge Entrance. Take the first right then the first right again before the golf kiosk car park.

AVON VALLEY RAILWAY

Address: Bitton Station, Bath Road, Bitton, Bristol BS30 6HD	**Nº of Steam Locos**: 6
Telephone Nº: (0117) 932-5538	**Nº of Other Locos**: 5
Year Formed: 1973	**Nº of Members**: Approximately 700
Location of Line: Midway between Bristol and Bath on A431	**Annual Membership Fee**: £15.00
	Approx Nº of Visitors P.A.: 80,000
	Gauge: Standard
Length of Line: 3 miles	**Web site**: www.avonvalleyrailway.org

GENERAL INFO

Nearest Mainline Station:
Keynsham (1½ miles)
Nearest Bus Station:
Bristol or Bath (7 miles)
Car Parking:
Available at Bitton Station
Coach Parking:
Available at Bitton Station
Souvenir Shop(s): Yes
Food & Drinks: Yes

SPECIAL INFO

The line has been extended through the scenic Avon Valley towards Bath and a new platform is now open linking with boat trips along the River Avon.

OPERATING INFO

Opening Times: Every Sunday and some Saturdays from Easter to October and on weekends during December. Also Bank Holiday Mondays, Wednesdays in June and July and Tuesdays to Thursdays during School Holidays. Also open for Santa Specials over Christmas. Open 10.30am to 5.00pm.
Steam Working:
11.00am to 4.00pm
Prices: Adult £6.00
Child £4.50
Family Tickets £16.50
Senior Citizens £5.00

Detailed Directions by Car:
From All Parts: Exit the M4 at Junction 18. Follow the A46 towards Bath and at the junction with the A420 turn right towards Bristol. At Bridge Yate turn left onto the A4175 and continue until you reach the A431. Turn right and Bitton Station is 100 yards on the right.

BALA LAKE RAILWAY

Address: Bala Lake Railway, Llanuwchllyn, Gwynedd, LL23 7DD **Telephone Nº**: (01678) 540666 **Year Formed**: 1972 **Location of Line**: Llanuwchllyn to Bala **Length of Line**: 4½ miles	**Nº of Steam Locos**: 5 (all are not in **Nº of Other Locos**: 3 working order) **Nº of Members**: – **Approx Nº of Visitors P.A.**: 20,000 **Gauge**: 1 foot 11 five-eighth inches **Web site**: www.bala-lake-railway.co.uk

GENERAL INFORMATION

Nearest Mainline Station: Wrexham (40 miles)
Nearest Bus Station: Wrexham (40 miles)
Car Parking: Adequate parking in Llanuwchllyn
Coach Parking: At Llanuwchllyn or in Bala Town Centre
Souvenir Shop(s): Yes
Food & Drinks: Yes – unlicensed!

SPECIAL INFORMATION

Bala Lake Railway is a narrow-gauge railway which follows 4½ miles of the former Ruabon to Barmouth G.W.R. line.

OPERATING INFORMATION

Opening Times: Easter until the end of September closed on Mondays and Fridays (excepting Bank Holidays) in April, May, June and September.
Steam Working: All advertised services are steam hauled. Trains run from 11.15am to 4.00pm.
Prices: Adult Single £6.50; Return £9.00
Child Single £2.50; Return £3.00
Senior Citizen Return £8.50
Family Tickets (Return): £11.00 (1 Adult + 1 Child); £22.00 (2 Adults + 2 Children). Additional Children pay £2.50 each.
Under 5's and dogs travel free of charge!

Detailed Directions by Car:
From All Parts: The railway is situated off the A494 Bala to Dolgellau road which is accessible from the national motorways via the A5 or A55.

BATH & WEST RAILWAY

Address: The Royal Bath and West Showground, Shepton Mallet, Somerset, BA4 6QN
Phone Nº: (01749) 840368 (Secretary)
Year Formed: 2001
Length of Line: ½ mile

Nº of Steam Locos: 7
Nº of Other Locos: 2
Nº of Members: Approximately 75
Annual Membership Fee: £28.00
Approx Nº of Visitors P.A.: 11,000
Gauge: 5 inches and 7¼ inches
Web site: www.essmee.org.uk

GENERAL INFORMATION

Nearest Mainline Station:
Castle Cary (4 miles)
Nearest Bus Station: –
Car Parking:
Free parking available on site
Coach Parking: Available
Food & Drinks:
Available during shows

SPECIAL INFORMATION

The Bath & West Railway is operated by members of the East Somerset Society of Model and Experimental Engineers.

OPERATING INFO

Opening Times: As the railway is situated on The Royal Bath and West Showground, operating days are governed by public access to the site. The railway operates on the four days of the Royal Bath & West Show at the end of May and the three days of The National Amateur Gardening Show early in September. Organisers of other shows have also asked the Society to operate the railway during their shows so please contact the Society for further dates. The Society's open weekend is to be held on 2nd & 3rd October 2010 when members of the public and other Engineering Societies are invited to visit.
Steam Working: All operating days.
Prices: Adults £1.50   Children £1.50

Detailed Directions by Car:
From All Parts: The Royal Bath and West Showground is situated approximately 2 miles south of Shepton Mallet just off the A371 road to Castle Cary.

BEER HEIGHTS LIGHT RAILWAY

Address: Pecorama, Beer, East Devon, EX12 3NA
Telephone Nº: (01297) 21542
Year Formed: 1975
Location of Line: Beer, East Devon
Length of Line: 1 mile

Nº of Steam Locos: 7 at present
Nº of Other Locos: 2
Nº of Members: –
Approx Nº of Visitors P.A.: 60,000
Gauge: 7¼ inches
Web site: www.peco-uk.com

GENERAL INFORMATION

Nearest Mainline Station: Axminster
Nearest Bus Stop: Beer
Car Parking: Available on site
Coach Parking: Available on site
Souvenir Shop(s): Yes
Food & Drinks: Licensed restaurant on site

SPECIAL INFORMATION

In addition to the Railway, Pecorama features a Model Railway Exhibition, childrens activity areas and extensive gardens.

OPERATING INFORMATION

Opening Times: 2010 dates: Weekdays 10.00am to 5.30pm and Saturdays 10.00am to 1.00pm from 29th March to 30th October. Also open on Sundays from Whitsun to the start of September from 10.00am to 5.30pm
Steam Working: Daily
Prices: Adult £7.00
Child £5.00 (Under-4s free of charge)
Senior Citizens £6.50 (Over-80s free)
Entrance to Pecorama includes one ride on the railway in the price.

Detailed Directions by Car:
From All Parts: Take the A3052 to Beer, turn onto the B3174 and follow the Brown Tourist signs for Pecorama.

BICKINGTON STEAM RAILWAY

Address: Trago Mills Shopping & Leisure Centre, Stover, Devon TQ12 6JB	**Nº of Steam Locos:** 4
Telephone Nº: (01626) 821111	**Nº of Other Locos:** 1
Year Formed: 1988	**Nº of Members:** None
Location of Line: Near the junction of A38 and A382	**Approx Nº of Visitors P.A.:** Not known
Length of Line: 1½ miles	**Gauge:** 10¼ inches
	Web site: None

GENERAL INFORMATION

Nearest Mainline Station: Newton Abbott (3½ miles)
Nearest Bus Station: Newton Abbott
Car Parking: Free parking available on site
Coach Parking: Available on site
Souvenir Shop(s): Yes
Food & Drinks: Available adjacent to the Railway

SPECIAL INFORMATION

Bickington Steam Railway is part of the Trago Mills Shopping & Leisure Centre which occupies around 100 acres of rolling South Devon countryside. The site has numerous other attractions including, 'The Finest 00-gauge Model Railway in the UK'!

OPERATING INFORMATION

Opening Times: Monday to Saturday 11.00am to 5.00pm and Sundays 12.00pm to 4.00pm.
Steam Working: Most operating days but please contact the Railway for precise information.
Prices: £4.99 for a Day Ticket which gives 10 rides.

Detailed Directions by Car:
From All Parts: Take the M5 from Exeter to the A38 and head towards Plymouth. Exit at the junction with the A382 and follow the signs for 'Trago Mills'. The railway is situated on this road after about 1 mile.

BICTON WOODLAND RAILWAY

Address: Bicton Woodland Railway, Bicton Park Botanical Gardens, East Budleigh, Budleigh Salterton   EX9 7OP
Telephone N°: (01395) 568465
Year Formed: 1963
Location of Line: Bicton Gardens
Length of Line: 1½ miles

N° of Steam Locos: None at present
N° of Other Locos: 3
N° of Members: 15,000
Annual Membership Fee: From £12.00
Approx N° of Visitors P.A.: 300,000
Gauge: 1 foot 6 inches
Web site: www.bictongardens.co.uk

GENERAL INFORMATION

Nearest Railtrack Station: Exmouth (6 miles)
Nearest Bus Station: Exeter (14 miles)
Car Parking: Free parking at site
Coach Parking: Free parking at site
Souvenir Shop(s): Yes
Food & Drinks: Yes

SPECIAL INFORMATION

The railway runs through the grounds of Bicton Park Botanical Gardens which span over 60 acres. The railway is the only 18 inch gauge line in the UK.

OPERATING INFORMATION

Opening Times: Daily 10.00am to 6.00pm during the Summer and 10.00am to 5.00pm during the Winter. Closed on Christmas Day and Boxing Day.
Steam Working: None at present
Prices: Adult £6.95 (Entrance);   £1.80 (Rides)
                 Child £5.95 (Entrance);   £1.30 (Rides)
Concessions £5.95 (Entrance);   £1.50 (Rides)

Detailed Directions by Car:
From All Parts: Exit the M5 motorway at Exeter services, Junction 30 and follow the brown tourist signs to Bicton Park.

BLISTS HILL CLAY MINE RAILWAY

Address: Blists Hill Victorian Town, Legges Way, Madeley, Telford TF7 5DU	**Nº of Steam Locos:** None
Telephone Nº: (01952) 601010	**Nº of Other Locos:** 1
Year Formed: 2009	**Nº of Members:** –
Location of Line: Telford, Shropshire	**Approx Nº of Visitors P.A.:** 200,000
Length of Line: 235 yards	**Gauge:** 2 feet
	Web site: www.ironbridge.org.uk

GENERAL INFORMATION

Nearest Mainline Station: Telford (6 miles)
Nearest Bus Station: Telford (6 miles)
Car Parking: Available on site
Coach Parking: Available
Souvenir Shop(s): Yes
Food & Drinks: Available

SPECIAL INFORMATION

The railway operates at Blists Hill Victorian Town which is one of the Ironbridge Gorge museums celebrating the birthplace of industry in England.

OPERATING INFORMATION

Opening Times: Daily throughout the year, generally from from 10.00am to 4.15pm although times may be subject to variation. Closed on Christmas Day and New Year's Day.
Steam Working: None at present.
Prices: Adults £2.00
       Children £1.50
       Family £6.00 (2 adults + 2 children)
Note: The above prices are for rides on the railway. Entrance to the Museum is an additional charge.

Detailed Directions by Car:
From All Parts: Exit the M54 at Junction 4 and head south on the Eastern Primary (A442) Road. Follow the Brown Tourist signs for Blists Hill Museum.

BODMIN & WENFORD RAILWAY

Address: Bodmin General Station, Losthwithiel Road, Bodmin, Cornwall PL31 1AQ	**N° of Steam Locos**: 11
	N° of Other Locos: 9
	N° of Members: 1,200
Telephone N°: (0845) 1259678	**Annual Membership Fee**: £14.00
Year Formed: 1984	**Approx N° of Visitors P.A.**: 53,000
Location of Line: Bodmin Parkway Station to Bodmin General & Boscarne Junction.	**Gauge**: Standard
	Web: www.bodminandwenfordrailway.co.uk
Length of Line: 6½ miles	

GENERAL INFORMATION

Nearest Mainline Station: Bodmin Parkway (cross platform interchange with the Bodmin & Wenford Railway)
Car Parking: Free parking at Bodmin General
Coach Parking: Free parking at Bodmin General
Souvenir Shop(s): Yes
Food & Drinks: Yes

SPECIAL INFORMATION

The Railway has steep gradients and there are two different branches to choose from Bodmin General. Through tickets to "Bodmin & Wenford Railway" are available from all Mainline stations.

OPERATING INFORMATION

Opening Times: 2010 dates: Daily from 29th May to 3rd October. Also daily during Easter week. Open other selected dates from February to May + October and Santa Specials on 4th, 5th, 11th, 12th, 18th, 19th, 24th, 26th, 27th, 28th & 31st December. Open 10.00am – 5.00pm on most days.
Steam Working: Most trains are steam-hauled except for most Saturdays when Diesels are used. Daily steam throughout August.
Prices: Adult All Day Rover £11.50
Child All Day Rover £6.00 (Under-3s free)
Family Day Rover £30.00
(2 adult + 2 child or 1 adult + 4 child)

Detailed Directions by Car:
From the A30/A38/A389 follow the signs to Bodmin Town Centre then follow the brown tourist signs to the Steam Railway on the B3268 Lostwithiel Road.

BRECON MOUNTAIN RAILWAY

Address: Pant Station, Dowlais, Merthyr Tydfil CF48 2UP	**Length of Line**: 5 miles (3½ in service)
Telephone Nº: (01685) 722988	**Nº of Steam Locos**: 8
Year Formed: 1980	**Nº of Other Locos**: 1
Location of Line: North of Merthyr Tydfil – 1 mile from the A465	**Nº of Members**: –
	Annual Membership Fee: –
Gauge: 1 foot 11¾ inches	**Approx Nº of Visitors P.A.**: 75,000
	Web: www.breconmountainrailway.co.uk

GENERAL INFORMATION

Nearest Mainline Station: Merthyr Tydfil (3 miles)
Nearest Bus Station: Merthyr Tydfil (3 miles)
Car Parking: Available at Pant Station
Coach Parking: Available at Pant Station
Souvenir Shop(s): Yes
Food & Drinks: Yes – including licensed restaurant

SPECIAL INFORMATION

It is possible to take a break before the return journey at Pontsticill to have a picnic, take a forest walk or visit the lakeside snackbar and play area.

OPERATING INFORMATION

Opening Times: Weekends and Bank Holidays throughout the year and daily during School holidays. Daily from the start of April to the end of October but closed on some Mondays and Fridays in April, May, September and October. Open almost every day in December for Santa Specials. Trains typically run from 11.00am to 4.55pm and from 12.00pm to 3.55pm during off-peak times.
Steam Working: Most services are steam hauled.
Prices: Adults £10.00
  Children £5.00 (Ages 2 and under ride free)
  Senior Citizens £9.25
Note: Two children can travel for £4.00 each when accompanying a paying adult.

Detailed Directions by Car:
Exit the M4 at Junction 32 and take the A470 to Merthyr Tydfil. Go onto the A465 and follow the brown tourist signs for the railway.

Bridgend & District m.e.s.

Address: Fountain Road, Tondu, Bridgend CF32 0EH	**N° of Steam Locos**: 6
Telephone N°: (01656) 740480	**N° of Other Locos**: 6
Year Formed: 1984	**N° of Members**: Approximately 45
Location of Line: Tondu, near Bridgend	**Approx N° of Visitors P.A.**: 800
Length of Line: 1,600 feet	**Gauge**: 3½ inches, 5 inches & 7¼ inches
	Web site: www.bdmes.org.uk

GENERAL INFORMATION

Nearest Mainline Station: Tondu (1 mile)
Nearest Bus Station: Bridgend (2 miles)
Car Parking: Available on site
Coach Parking: Available on site
Food & Drinks: Available

OPERATING INFORMATION

Opening Times: The first Saturday and 3rd Sunday of each month from April to October inclusive. Also on Bank Holiday Mondays. Please contact the railway for further details. Trains run from noon until 4.00pm.
Steam Working: All open days where possible.
Prices: 60p per person per ride.
Note: The line is available for birthday party bookings. Please contact the Society for details.

Detailed Directions by Car:
Exit the M4 at Junction 36 and follow the A4063 Northwards. At the first roundabout take the 2nd exit onto the B4281 Park Road. Continue into Fountain Road and turn right (still on Fountain Road). The MES club area is located on the right just before the crossroads.

BRISTOL HARBOUR RAILWAY

Address: Princes Wharf, City Docks, Bristol BS1 4RN	**Nº of Steam Locos:** 2
Telephone Nº: (0117) 903-1570	**Nº of Other Locos:** 1
Year Formed: 1978	**Nº of Members:** –
Location of Line: South side of the Floating Harbour	**Annual Membership Fee:** –
	Approx Nº of Visitors P.A.: –
	Gauge: Standard
Length of Line: 1½ miles	**Web site:** None

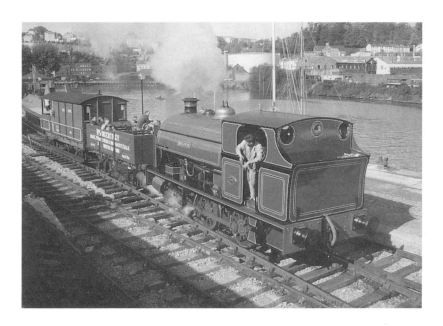

GENERAL INFORMATION

Nearest Mainline Station: Bristol Temple Meads (1 mile)
Nearest Bus Station: City Centre (½ mile)
Car Parking: None at present
Coach Parking: None at present
Souvenir Shop(s): None at present
Food & Drinks: Cafes available near the Railway

SPECIAL INFORMATION

Although the Bristol Industrial Museum is currently closed, the railway continues to operate on a limited basis between S.S. Great Britain and Cumberland Basin during 2010. Platforms are located at the Create Centre and the SS Great Britain.

OPERATING INFORMATION

Opening Times: 2010 dates: 20th & 21st March; 3rd, 4th, 5th, 17th & 18th April; 1st, 2nd, 3rd, 29th, 30th & 21st May; 19th & 20th June; 10th, 11th & 31st July; 1st, 28th, 29th & 30th August; 11th & 12th September; 2nd, 3rd, 23rd, 24th, 30th & 31st October. Trains run from 11.00am to 5.00pm.
Steam Working: Please contact the railway for further details.
Prices: Return £3.00
　　　　　 Single £2.00
Note: Children under the age of 6 travel for free.

Detailed Directions by Car:
From All Parts: Follow signs to Bristol City Centre and then the Brown Tourist signs for the Museum. A good landmark to look out for are the 4 huge quayside cranes.

BROOMY HILL RAILWAY

Address: Broomy Hill, Hereford	**Nº of Steam Locos**: 4+
Telephone Nº: (01989) 762119	**Nº of Other Locos**: 1+
Year Formed: 1962	**Nº of Members**: Approximately 80
Location of Line: Adjacent to the	**Approx Nº of Visitors P.A.**: Not known
Waterworks Museum, Hereford	**Gauge**: 7¼ inches, 5 inches, 3½ inches
Length of Line: 1 kilometre	**Web site**: www.hsme.co.uk

GENERAL INFORMATION

Nearest Mainline Station: Hereford (1½ miles)
Nearest Bus Station: Hereford (1½ miles)
Car Parking: Free parking available on site
Coach Parking: Available by prior arrangement
Souvenir Shop(s): Yes
Food & Drinks: Available

SPECIAL INFORMATION

The Broomy Hill Railway is operated by the Hereford Society of Model Engineers and has two separate tracks which run along the bank of the River Wye. Members run their own locomotives so the number and variety in operation may vary from day to day. Entry to the site is free of charge and picnic areas are available.

OPERATING INFORMATION

Opening Times: The second and last Sundays of the month from Easter until September/October. Trains run from 12.00pm to 4.30pm.
Steam Working: All operating days.
Prices: Adults £1.50 per ride
Children £1.50 per ride
Note: Four rides can be bought for £5.00

Detailed Directions by Car:
From the centre of Hereford, take the A49 Ross-on-Wye Road, turning right into Barton Road. After approximately 400 metres, turn left into Broomy Hill Road, proceed for around 600 metres before turning left following signs for the Waterworks Museum. The railway is on the right just after the museum which is signposted with Brown Tourist Information Signs.

CAMBRIAN HERITAGE RAILWAYS

Address: Cambrian Railways Trust, Llynclys South Station, Llynclys, Oswestry, Shropshire SY10 8BX	**N° of Steam Locos**: 2 (1 in operation)
	N° of Other Locos: 2
	N° of Members: 200+
Telephone N°: (01691) 679007	**Annual Membership Fee**: £12.00
Year Formed: 1997	**Approx N° of Visitors P.A.**: 2,500
Location of Line: Llynclys, Oswestry	**Gauge**: Standard
Length of Line: Approximately ¾ mile	**Web site**: www.cambrianrailways.com

GENERAL INFORMATION

Nearest Mainline Station: Gobowen (7 miles)
Nearest Bus Station: Oswestry (5 miles)
Car Parking: Limited parking available on site
Coach Parking: Limited park available on site
Souvenir Shop(s): Yes
Food & Drinks: Available

SPECIAL INFORMATION

In 2007, the Cambrian Railway Trust ran their first steam service. This was the first steam train on the line for more than 40 years! The Trust ultimately aims to extend the line to run a regular passenger service from Llynclys wharf to Pen-y-Garreg Lane.

OPERATING INFORMATION

Opening Times: 2010 dates: Open every Saturday, Sunday and Bank Holiday from Easter to the 26th September. Also open on Sundays in October and December. Trains run from 11.00am to 4.00pm.
Steam Working: Please contact the Railway for information.
Prices: Adults £4.50 (Steam) £2.50 (Diesel)
Concessions £2.50 (Steam) £1.00 (Diesel)
Family £12.00 (Steam) £6.00 (Diesel)
Note: All the above are "Full Day Rover" tickets.

Detailed Directions by Car:
The Railway is situated on the B4396 approximately 5 miles southwest of Oswestry, just off the A483 heading towards Welshpool. Turn left at Llyncly Crossroads towards Knockin. The entrance to the site is on the right after about 400 yards, immediately over the railway bridge.

CARDIFF MODEL ENGINEERING SOCIETY

Address: Heath Park, King George V
Drive, Cardiff   CF14 4EN
Telephone Nº: None
Year Formed: 1948
Location of Line: Heath Park, Cardiff
Length of Line: 2 tracks of 1,000 feet
each plus a tram track of 700 feet

Nº of Steam Locos: 8
Nº of Other Locos: 4
Nº of Members: Approximately 150
Approx Nº of Visitors P.A.: 7,000
Gauge: 3½ inches, 5 inches & 7¼ inches
Web site: www.cardiffmes.com

GENERAL INFORMATION

Nearest Mainline Station: Heath Low Level (½ mile)
Nearest Bus Station: Cardiff
Car Parking: Available on site and also nearby
Coach Parking: None
Food & Drinks: Available

SPECIAL INFORMATION

The Cardiff Model Engineering society moved to
Heath Park in 1987. The site, which includes two
railway tracks and a unique electric tramway, two
model railways, and extensive refreshment facilities,
has been developed by the members for the benefit
of visitors.

OPERATING INFORMATION

Opening Times: 2010 public dates: 4th & 6th April;
30th & 31st May; 27th June; 25th July; 29th & 30th
August; 12th September; 3rd & 24th October. Also
a ticket-only Santa special service on 5th December.
Trains run from 1.00pm to 5.00pm.
Steam Working: All operating days.
Prices: £1.50 entry per person then £1.20 per ride.
Children aged 3 and under are admitted and ride
free of charge.
Please note that prices may be subject to change.

Detailed Directions by Car:
Exit the M4 at Junction 32 and travel towards Cardiff. Turn left at the 3rd set of traffic lights (by the Tesco garage)
and continue through 3 sets of traffic lights to the T-junction lights. Turn left here then immediately right then
take the 1st left onto King George V Drive. Turn left at the roundabout and take the lane 400 yards on the right.

THE CATTLE COUNTRY RAILWAY

Address: Cattle Country Adventure Park, Berkeley Heath Farm, Berkeley, Glos, GL13 9EW
Telephone Nº: (01453) 810510
Year Formed: 2005
Location of Line: Berkeley Heath
Length of Line: ½ mile

Nº of Steam Locos: None at present
Nº of Other Locos: 1
Approx Nº of Visitors P.A.: 100,000
Gauge: 10¼ inches
Web site: www.cattlecountry.co.uk

GENERAL INFORMATION

Nearest Mainline Station: Cam & Dursley (5 miles)
Car Parking: Free parking available on site
Coach Parking: Free parking available on site
Souvenir Shop(s): Yes
Food & Drinks: Yes

SPECIAL INFORMATION

The railway runs through the Cattle Country Adventure Park which hosts a wide variety of attractions for all the family. Entrance fees to the Park vary depending on the time of the year. Details can be found on: www.cattlecountry.co.uk

OPERATING INFORMATION

Opening Times: 2010 dates: Open on Sundays from mid-February to the end of October. Also open on Saturdays from Easter to the end of August, daily from 3rd July to 3rd September and at various other dates in the School Holidays. Please contact the Park for further details. Open 10.00am to 4.00pm (5.00pm in the Summer).
Steam Working: None at present.
Prices: Adult Return £1.50 (Single £1.00)
Child Return £1.00 (Single 75p)
Note: Admission charges for the Cattle Country Adventure Park are an additional charge.

Detailed Directions by Car:
From the North: Exit the M5 at Junction 13 and join the A38 travelling towards Bristol. After 8 miles you reach Berkeley Heath, turn right past the garage and follow the brown tourist signs for Cattle Country; From the South: Exit the M5 at Junction 14 and take the A38 towards Gloucester. After approximately 6 miles turn left following the brown tourist signs for Cattle Country.

COATE WATER PARK MINIATURE RAILWAY

Address: Coate Water Country Park, Swindon, Wiltshire   SN3 6AA
Telephone N°: (01666) 577596 (Secretary)
Year Formed: 1964
Location of Line: Coate Water Country Park, Swindon
Length of Line: ½ mile

N° of Steam/Other Locos: A number of different locos are supplied for use by members of the Society
N° of Members: Approximately 70
Approx N° of Visitors P.A.: Not known
Gauge: 5 inches and 7¼ inches

GENERAL INFORMATION

Nearest Mainline Station: Swindon (2 miles)
Nearest Bus Station: Swindon (2 miles)
Car Parking: Available in the Park
Coach Parking: None
Food & Drinks: Available in the Park

SPECIAL INFORMATION

The Coate Water Park Miniature Railway is operated by volunteers from the North Wiltshire Model Engineering Society.

OPERATING INFORMATION

Opening Times: Sundays (weather permitting). Open from 11.00am with trains running until approximately 5.00pm.
Steam Working: Depends which locos have been provided for use on the day by the individual members.
Prices: £1.00 per person per ride.

Detailed Directions by Car:
From Junction 15 of the M4, take the A419 North. Take the first exit left onto the A4259 towards Swindon and follow the dual-carriageway past the Great Western Hospital then turn left at the roundabout for Coate Water Park and follow the road to the main car park. From the car park walk round to the left for the railway.

COLEFORD GWR MUSEUM

Address: The Old Railway Station, Railway Drive, Coleford GL16 8RH
Telephone Nº: (01594) 833569
Year Formed: 1988
Location of Line: Coleford
Length of Line: 100 yards

Nº of Steam Locos: 2
Nº of Other Locos: –
Nº of Members: –
Approx Nº of Visitors P.A.: Not known
Gauge: 7¼ inches and Standard gauge
Web site: www.colefordgwr.150m.com

GENERAL INFORMATION

Nearest Mainline Station: Lydney (7½ miles)
Nearest Bus Station: Gloucester (20 miles)
Car Parking: Available on site
Coach Parking: Available on site
Souvenir Shop(s): Yes
Food & Drinks: Tea and Coffee available only

SPECIAL INFORMATION

Based in the 1883 Goods Shed at Coleford, the Museum chronicles the history of railways in the Forest of Dean.

OPERATING INFORMATION

Opening Times: Friday and Saturday afternoons and Bank Holidays throughout the year. Open from 2.30pm to 5.00pm and at other times by prior arrangement.
Steam Working: Easter Monday and other Bank Holidays. Please contact the Museum for details.
Prices: Adults £3.00 (admission to the museum)
Children £1.50 (admission to the museum)
Miniature Railway Rides £1.50
Peckett Footplate Visit £2.00 (if steaming)

Detailed Directions by Car:
From All Parts: From the M50 take the A40 at Ross-on-Wye to Monmouth then the A4136 towards Cinderford. Turn off the A4136 into Coleford and the Museum is located in the Town Centre.

COMBE MARTIN WILDLIFE PARK RAILWAY

Address: Higher Leigh, Combe Martin, EX34 0NG
Telephone Nº: (01271) 882486
Year Formed: 1989
Location of Line: North Devon
Length of Line: 500 yards

Nº of Steam Locos: None
Nº of Other Locos: 1
Nº of Members: –
Approx Nº of Visitors P.A.: 100,000 (to the Wildlife Park)
Gauge: 15 inches
Web site: www.dinosaur-park.com

GENERAL INFORMATION

Nearest Mainline Station: Barnstaple (13 miles)
Nearest Bus Station: Barnstaple (13 miles)
Car Parking: Available on site
Coach Parking: Available
Souvenir Shop(s): Yes
Food & Drinks: Available

SPECIAL INFORMATION

In addition to the railway, Combe Martin Wildlife & Dinosaur Park offers a wide range of attractions for all the family.

OPERATING INFORMATION

Opening Times: 2010 Dates: Daily from 13th February to 7th November. Trains operate from 12.00pm to 4.30pm.
Steam Working: None at present.
Prices: Adults £14.00 (Admission to Park)
Children £8.50 (Admission to Park)
Concessions £10.00 (Admission to Park)
Family £40.00 (Admission to Park)
Note: Train rides are an extra £1.00 per person.

Detailed Directions by Car:
From All Parts: Take the A399 to Combe Martin and the Park is situated by the side of the road near the Kentisbury crossroads.

CONWY VALLEY RAILWAY MUSEUM

Address: Old Goods Yard, Betws-y-Coed, Conwy, North Wales LL24 0AL	**Nº of Steam Locos:** 4
	Nº of Other Locos: 2
Telephone Nº: (01690) 710568	**Nº of Members:** –
Year Formed: 1983	**Annual Membership Fee:** –
Location of Line: Betws-y-Coed	**Approx Nº of Visitors P.A.:** 50,000
Length of Line: One and an eighth miles	**Gauge:** 7¼ inches and 15 inches
	Web site: www.conwyrailwaymuseum.co.uk

GENERAL INFORMATION

Nearest Mainline Station: Betws-y-Coed (20 yards)
Nearest Bus Station: 40 yards
Car Parking: Car park at site
Coach Parking: Car park at site
Souvenir Shop(s): Yes
Food & Drinks: Yes – Buffet Coach Cafe

SPECIAL INFORMATION

The Museum houses the unique 3D dioramas by the late Jack Nelson. Also the ¼ size steam loco 'Britannia'. The railway has rebuilt two Denver and Rio Grande C16 locomotives for use on the line. It also operated an Isle of Man loco – "Douglas".

OPERATING INFORMATION

Opening Times: Daily from 10.00am to 5.00pm.
Trains Working: Daily from 10.15am
Prices: Adult – £1.50 museum entry;
Train rides £1.50; Tram rides £1.00
Child/Senior Citizen – 80p museum entry;
Train rides £1.50; Tram rides £1.00
Family tickets – £4.00

Detailed Directions by Car:
From Midlands & South: Take M54/M6 onto the A5 and into Betws-y-Coed; From Other Parts: Take the A55 coast road then the A470 to Betws-y-Coed. The museum is located by the Mainline Station directly off the A5.

THE CORRIS RAILWAY

Address: Station Yard, Corris, Machynlleth, Mid Wales SY20 9SH	**Nº of Steam Locos**: 1
Telephone Nº: (01654) 761303	**Nº of Other Locos**: 4
Year Formed: 1966	**Nº of Members**: 500
Location of Line: Corris to Maespoeth, Mid Wales	**Annual Membership Fee**: £15.00 (adult)
	Approx Nº of Visitors P.A.: 7,000
Length of Line: ¾ mile	**Gauge**: 2 feet 3 inches
	Web site: www.corris.co.uk

GENERAL INFORMATION

Nearest Mainline Station: Machynlleth (5 miles)
Nearest Bus Station: Machynlleth (5 miles)
Car Parking: Available on site and also at the Corris Craft Centre (500 yards)
Coach Parking: Corris Craft Centre (please pre-book if visiting)
Souvenir Shop(s): Yes
Food & Drinks: Yes

SPECIAL INFORMATION

The Corris Railway Society was formed in 1966 and the line itself dates back to 1859. The Railway's new-build 'Tattoo' class steam locomotive was delivered on 17th May 2005.

OPERATING INFORMATION

Opening Times: 2010 dates: Open over the Easter weekend and then every Sunday from May until the end of September, Saturdays in July and August and Mondays and Tuesdays from 26th July to 30th August, plus Bank Holiday weekends. The first train leaves Corris Station at 11.00am, last train at 4.00pm
Steam Working: Most trains are steam-hauled.
Prices: Adult Return £5.00
Child Return £2.50
Senior Citizen Return £4.50
Family Return £12.50
(2 adults + 2 children)

Detailed Directions by Car:
From All Parts: Corris is situated off the A487 trunk road, five miles north of Machynlleth and 11 miles south of Dolgellau. Turn off the trunk road at the Braichgoch Hotel and the Station Yard is the 2nd turn on the right as you enter the village, just past the Holy Trinity Church.

THE DARTMOOR RAILWAY

Address: Okehampton Station, Station Road, Okehampton EX20 1EJ **Telephone Nº**: (01837) 55164 **Year Formed**: 1997 **Location of Line**: Meldon Quarry to Coleford Junction	**Length of Line**: 15½ miles **Nº of Steam Locos**: Visiting locos only **Nº of Other Locos**: 1 and DMUs **Gauge**: Standard **Web site**: www.dartmoor-railway.co.uk

GENERAL INFORMATION

Nearest Mainline Station: Crediton
Nearest Bus Station: Okehampton
Car Parking: Okehampton Station and some spaces at Sampford Courtenay Station – all free of charge
Coach Parking: Okehampton Station
Souvenir Shop(s): Yes
Food & Drinks: Okehampton Buffet is open from Friday to Sunday throughout the year. The Buffet is fully licensed.

SPECIAL INFORMATION

The railway operates on the route of the old Southern Railway line through the mid-Devon countryside to the northern slopes of Dartmoor National Park.

OPERATING INFORMATION

Opening Times: Weekends and daily during the School Holidays from Easter until the end of September. Please contact the railway for details.
Steam Working: Visiting locomotives only. Please contact the railway for further information.
Prices: Vary depending upon the destination. Please contact the railway for further information.
Note: Commuter services through to Exeter are planned from 23rd May 2010.

Detailed Directions by Car:
From All Parts: Take the A30 Exeter to Launceston dual carriageway and exit at the Okehampton turn-off. Once in town, follow the brown tourist signs up the hill to Okehampton Station.

DEVON RAILWAY CENTRE

Address: Bickleigh, Tiverton, Devon, EX16 8RG
Telephone Nº: (01884) 855671
Year Formed: 1997
Location of Line: Bickleigh, Devon
Length of Line: ½ mile (2 foot and 7¼ inch gauges); 200 yards (Standard gauge)

Nº of Steam Locos: 3
Nº of Other Locos: 19
Nº of Members: None
Approx Nº of Visitors P.A.: −
Gauge: 2 feet, 7¼ inches and Standard
Web site: www.devonrailwaycentre.co.uk

GENERAL INFORMATION

Nearest Mainline Station: Exeter
Nearest Bus Station: Tiverton (Route 55)
Car Parking: Available on site
Coach Parking: Available on site
Souvenir Shop(s): Yes
Food & Drinks: Yes

SPECIAL INFORMATION

Devon Railway Centre has passenger carrying lines and also features a large model railway exhibition with 15 working layouts. A delightful Edwardian model village has recently been built to a 1:12 scale and there are indoor and outdoor play areas.

OPERATING INFORMATION

Opening Times: 2010 dates: Daily from 2nd to 18th April, 5th May to 26th September and 23rd to 31st October. Closed on Mondays (but not Bank Holidays) during May, June and September and also on Tuesdays in May and September. Santa Specials run on 11th, 12th, 18th & 19th December. Open from 10.30am until 5.00pm on all operating days.
Steam Working: Trains may be steam or diesel hauled so please phone for further details.
Prices: Adult £6.40   Child £5.10
      Senior Citizen £5.30   Family £20.30
Admission includes unlimited train rides and access to the model village, model railways and museum.

Detailed Directions by Car:
From All Parts: Devon Railway Centre is situated adjacent to the famous Bickleigh Bridge, just off the A396 Exeter to Tiverton road (3 miles from Tiverton and 8 miles from Exeter).

DEAN FOREST RAILWAY

Address: Norchard Centre, Forest Road; Lydney, Gloucestershire GL15 4ET
Telephone Nº: (01594) 845840
Information Line: (01594) 843423 (24 hr.)
Year Formed: 1970
Location of Line: Lydney, Gloucestershire
Length of Line: 4½ miles

Nº of Steam Locos: 7 (4 working)
Nº of Other Locos: 18
Nº of Members: 1,000
Annual Membership Fee: Adult £14.00; Family (4 persons) £17.00
Approx Nº of Visitors P.A.: 35,000
Gauge: Standard
Web site: www.deanforestrailway.co.uk

GENERAL INFORMATION

Nearest Mainline Station: Lydney (200 metres)
Nearest Bus Station: Lydney Town (400 metres)
Car Parking: 600 spaces available at Norchard
Coach Parking: Ample space available
Souvenir Shop(s): Yes + a Museum
Food & Drinks: Yes – on operational days only

SPECIAL INFORMATION

Dean Forest Railway preserves the sole surviving line of the Severn and Wye Railway. The Railway has lengthened the line to a total of 4½ miles and Norchard to Parkend is now open for steam train operation giving a round trip of 9 miles.

OPERATING INFORMATION

Opening Times: 2010 dates: Norchard is open every day for viewing. Trains operate on Sundays from March to the end of October, on Wednesdays and Saturdays from 4th June to 26th September, Thursdays in August and various other dates. Phone or check the railway's web site for further details.
Steam Working: Most services are steam-hauled – check the web site or phone for details. Trains depart Norchard at various times from 10.35am to 3.30pm.
Prices: Adult Return £10.00
Child Return £5.00 (ages 5-16 years old)
Family Tickets £28.00
Note: Fares may differ on Special Event days.

Detailed Directions by Car:
From M50 & Ross-on-Wye: Take the B4228 and B4234 via Coleford to reach Lydney. Norchard is located on the B4234, ¾ mile north of Lydney Town Centre; From Monmouth: Take the A4136 and B4431 onto the B4234 via Coleford; From South Wales: Take the M4 then M48 onto the A48 via Chepstow to Lydney; From Midlands/Gloucester: Take the M5 to Gloucester then the A48 to Lydney; From the West Country: Take the M4 and M48 via the 'Old' Severn Bridge to Chepstow and then the A48 to Lydney.

EASTLEIGH LAKESIDE STEAM RAILWAY

Address: Lakeside Country Park, Wide Lane, Eastleigh, Hants. SO50 5PE	**N° of Steam Locos**: 18
Telephone N°: (023) 8061-2020	**N° of Other Locos**: 3
Year Formed: 1992	**N° of Members**: –
Location: Opposite Southampton airport	**Approx N° of Visitors P.A.**: 50,000
Length of Line: 1¼ miles	**Gauge**: 10¼ inches and 7¼ inches
	Web site: www.steamtrain.co.uk

GENERAL INFORMATION

Nearest Mainline Station: Southampton Airport (Parkway) (¼ mile)
Nearest Bus Station: Eastleigh (1½ miles)
Car Parking: Free parking available on site
Coach Parking: Free parking available on site
Souvenir Shop(s): Yes
Food & Drinks: Cafe on site when railway is open

SPECIAL INFORMATION

The railway also has a playground and picnic area overlooking the lakes.

OPERATING INFORMATION

Opening Times: Weekends throughout the year and daily from mid-July until mid-September plus all other school holidays. Open 10.00am to 4.30pm (until 4.00pm during the winter months). Santa Specials run on some dates in December.
Steam Working: As above
Prices: Adult Return £3.00 (First Class £3.50)
Child Return £2.50 (First Class £3.00)
Tickets are available offering 3 return journeys at reduced rates. Annual season tickets are available. Children under the age of 2 years ride free of charge. Driver training courses can be booked in advance.

Detailed Directions by Car:
From All Parts: Exit the M27 at Junction 5 and take the A335 to Eastleigh. The Railway is situated ¼ mile past Southampton Airport Station on the left hand side of the A335.

EAST SOMERSET RAILWAY (STRAWBERRY LINE)

Address: Cranmore Railway Station, Shepton Mallet, Somerset   BA4 4QP
Telephone N°: (01749) 880417
Year Formed: 1971
Location of Line: Cranmore, off A361 between Frome and Shepton Mallet
Length of Line: 3 miles

N° of Steam Locos: 5
N° of Other Locos: 2
N° of Members: 480
Annual Season Ticket Fee: Single £30.00
Family £80.00
Approx N° of Visitors P.A.: 20,000
Gauge: Standard

GENERAL INFORMATION

Nearest Mainline Station: Castle Cary (10 miles)
Nearest Bus Station: Shepton Mallet (3 miles)
Car Parking: Space for 100 cars available
Coach Parking: Available by arrangement
Souvenir Shop(s): Yes
Food & Drinks: Yes

SPECIAL INFORMATION

Footplate experience courses available – phone (01749) 880417 for further details.

Web site: www.eastsomersetrailway.com

OPERATING INFORMATION

Opening Times: Complex, Museum and Engine Sheds open daily from April to December and Tuesdays, Thursdays, Saturdays, January to March. Closed on Mondays and Wednesdays in November.
Steam Working: 2010 dates: Weekends and Bank Holidays from 3rd April to September, Wednesdays from June to August and Thursdays in August. Santa Specials run on some December weekends. Special events on other dates. Open 10.00am to 4.00pm (5.30pm in the Summer).
Prices: Adult Return £7.50   Child Return £5.50
Senior Citizen Return £6.50   Family Return £22.00

Detailed Directions by Car:
From the North: Take A367/A37 to Shepton Mallet then turn left onto A361 to Frome. Carry on to Shepton Mallet and 9 miles after Frome turn left at Cranmore; From the South: Take A36 to Frome bypass then A361 to Cranmore; From the West: Take A371 from Wells to Shepton Mallet, then A361 to Frome (then as above).

EXBURY GARDENS RAILWAY

Address: Exbury Gardens, Exbury,
Near Southampton   SO45 1AZ
Telephone Nº: (02380) 891203
Year Formed: 2001
Location of Line: Exbury
Length of Line: 1½ miles

Nº of Steam Locos: 3
Nº of Other Locos: 1
Nº of Members: None
Approx Nº of Visitors P.A.: 55,000
Gauge: 12¼ inches
Web site: www.exbury.co.uk

GENERAL INFORMATION

Nearest Mainline Station: Brockenhurst (8 miles)
Nearest Bus Station: Hill Top (2½ miles)
Car Parking: Free parking available on site
Coach Parking: Free parking available on site
Souvenir Shop(s): Yes
Food & Drinks: Available

SPECIAL INFORMATION

The railway is located in the world famous Rothschild azalea and rhododendron gardens at Exbury in the New Forest. A walk-through exhibition is scheduled to open during the Spring of 2010.

OPERATING INFORMATION

Opening Times: 2010 dates: Daily from the 13th March to 7th November. Also open for Santa Specials on 11th, 12th, 18th, 19th, 20th & 21st December. Open from 10.00am to 5.00pm (or dusk if earlier).
Steam Working: Most running days from 11.00am (restricted operation in March and September).
Prices: Adult Return   £3.50
                Child Return   £3.50
Note: Day Rover tickets are available during the low season for an additional £1.00 charge.

Detailed Directions by Car:
From all directions: Exit the M27 at Junction 2 and take the A326 to Dibden. Follow the brown tourist signs for Exbury Gardens & Steam Railway.

EXMOUTH EXPRESS

Address: Queen's Drive, Exmouth, EX8 2AY	**Nº of Steam Locos**: None
Telephone Nº: (01395) 222545	**Nº of Other Locos**: 1
Year Formed: 1949	**Nº of Members**: –
Location of Line:	**Approx Nº of Visitors P.A.**: Not known
Length of Line: 150 yards	**Gauge**: 10¼ inches
	Web site: None

Photo courtesy of Jonathan James

GENERAL INFORMATION

Nearest Mainline Station: Exmouth (½ mile)
Nearest Bus Station: Exmouth (½ mile)
Car Parking: Available on site
Coach Parking: Available
Souvenir Shop(s): Yes
Food & Drinks: Available

SPECIAL INFORMATION

The Exmouth Express is one of the oldest seaside railways of its type.

OPERATING INFORMATION

Opening Times: Daily from Easter until the end of September. Trains run from 10.00am to 6.00pm.
Steam Working: None at present.
Prices: Adults £1.50
Children 50p

Detailed Directions by Car:
From All Parts: Take the A376 to Exmouth and continue through to the beach for Queen's Drive.

FAIRBOURNE RAILWAY

Address: Beach Road, Fairbourne, Dolgellau, Gwynedd LL38 2EX	**Nº of Steam Locos**: 4
Telephone Nº: (01341) 250362	**Nº of Other Locos**: 2
Year Formed: 1916	**Nº of Members**: 197
Location of Line: On A493 between Tywyn & Dolgellau	**Annual Membership Fee**: £25.00
Length of Line: 2 miles	**Approx Nº of Visitors P.A.**: 18,000
	Gauge: 12¼ inches
	Web Site: www.fairbournerailway.com

GENERAL INFORMATION

Nearest Mainline Station: Fairbourne (adjacent)
Nearest Bus Station: Fairbourne (adjacent)
Car Parking: Available in Mainline station car park
Coach Parking: Pay & Display car park 300 yards (the Railway will re-imburse car parking charges for party bookings)
Souvenir Shop(s): Yes
Food & Drinks: Yes – Tea room at Fairbourne, Cafe at Barmouth Ferry Terminus

SPECIAL INFORMATION

There is a connecting ferry service (foot passengers only) from Barmouth to Barmouth Ferry Terminus.

OPERATING INFORMATION

Opening Times: 2010 dates: Open over Easter Holiday week then daily from 1st May to 19th September (closed on Mondays and Fridays except from mid-July to the end of August). Open at weekends until 24th October then daily from 25th to 31st October. Santa Specials run on 18th and 19th December at 11.30am and 1.30pm.
Steam Working: 11.00am to 3.30pm for normal service. At peak times 10.40am to 4.20pm.
Prices: Adult Return £7.80
Child Return £4.20
Family £18.95 (2 adults + up to 3 children)
Senior Citizen Return £6.50

Detailed Directions by Car:
From A470: Follow signs for Dolgellau and turn left onto A493 towards Tywyn. The turn-off for Fairbourne is located 8 miles south-west of Dolgellau; From South Wales: Follow signs for Machynlleth, then follow A487 towards Dolgellau. Then take A493 towards Fairbourne.

FFESTINIOG RAILWAY

Address: Ffestiniog Railway, Harbour Station, Porthmadog, Gwynedd LL49 9NF	**N° of Steam Locos:** 12
Telephone N°: (01766) 516000	**N° of Other Locos:** 12
Year Formed: 1832	**N° of Members:** 5,000
Location of Line: Porthmadog to Blaenau Ffestiniog	**Annual Membership Fee:** £22.00
Length of Line: 13½ miles	**Approx N° of Visitors P.A.:** 140,000
	Gauge: 1 foot 11½ inches
	Web Site: www.festrail.co.uk

GENERAL INFORMATION

Nearest Mainline Station: Blaenau Ffestiniog (interchange) or Minffordd
Nearest Bus Station: Bus stop next to stations at Porthmadog & Blaenau Ffestiniog
Car Parking: Parking available at Porthmadog, Blaenau Ffestiniog, Minffordd and Tan-y-Bwlch
Coach Parking: Available at Porthmadog and Blaenau Ffestiniog
Souvenir Shop(s): Yes
Food & Drinks: Yes

SPECIAL INFORMATION

The Railway runs through the spectacular scenery of Snowdonia National Park and, from 2011 the line is scheduled to link up with the Welsh Highland Railway.

OPERATING INFORMATION

Opening Times: Daily service from late March to early November. A limited service operates in the Winter. Please contact the railway for further details.
Steam Working: Most trains are steam hauled.
Prices: Adult £17.95 (All-day Rover ticket)
One child travels free with each adult, additional children travel for half the fare.
Reductions are available for Senior Citizens and groups of 20 or more.
Cheaper fares are also available for single rides and shorter journeys.

Detailed Directions by Car:
Portmadog is easily accessible from the Midlands – take the M54/A5 to Corwen then the A494 to Bala onto the A4212 to Trawsfynydd and the A470 (becomes the A487 from Maentwrog) to Porthmadog. From Chester take the A55 to Llandudno Junction and the A470 to Blaenau Ffestiniog. Both Stations are well-signposted.

GARTELL LIGHT RAILWAY

Address: Common Lane, Yenston,
Templecombe, Somerset   BA8 0NB
Telephone N°: (01963) 370752
Year Formed: 1991
Location of Line: South of Templecombe
Length of Line: ¾ mile

N° of Steam Locos: 2
N° of Other Locos: 3
Approx N° of Visitors P.A.: 3,000
Gauge: 2 feet
Web site: www.glr-online.co.uk

GENERAL INFORMATION

Nearest Mainline Station: Templecombe (1¼ miles)
Nearest Bus Station: Wincanton
Car Parking: Free parking adjacent to the station
Coach Parking: Adjacent to the station
Souvenir Shop(s): Yes
Food & Drinks: Meals, snacks and drinks available

SPECIAL INFORMATION

The railway is fully signalled using a variety of
semaphore, colour-light and shunting signals,
controlled by signalmen in two operational signal
boxes. Part of the line runs along the track bed of
the old Somerset & Dorset Joint Railway.

OPERATING INFORMATION

Opening Times: 2010 dates: 5th April; 3rd May;
31st May; 27th June; 24th/25th July (Steam Rally);
1st, 8th, 15th, 22nd, 29th & 30th August;
26th September and 24th October. Pre-booked Santa
Specials run on 11th & 12th December.
Trains depart at frequent intervals between 10.30am
and 4.30pm.
Steam Working: Every day the railway operates.
Prices: Adult £7.00
            Senior Citizen £5.50
            Child £3.50
Note: Tickets permit unlimited travel by any train
on the day of purchase. Under-5s travel for free.

Detailed Directions by Car:
From All Parts: The Railway is situated off the A357 just south of Templecombe and on open days is clearly
indicated by the usual brown tourist signs.

GLOUCESTERSHIRE WARWICKSHIRE RAILWAY

Address: The Station, Toddington, Cheltenham, Gloucestershire GL54 5DT	**Nº of Steam Locos**: 11
Telephone Nº: (01242) 621405	**Nº of Other Locos**: 17
Year Formed: 1981	**Nº of Members**: 3,500
Location of Line: 5 miles south of Broadway, Worcestershire, near the A46	**Annual Membership Fee**: £16.00 (Adult)
Length of Line: 10 miles	**Approx Nº of Visitors P.A.**: 70,000
	Gauge: Standard and Narrow gauge
	Web site: www.gwsr.com

GENERAL INFORMATION

Nearest Mainline Station: Cheltenham Spa or Ashchurch
Nearest Bus Station: Cheltenham
Car Parking: Parking available at Toddington, Winchcombe & Cheltenham Racecourse Stations
Coach Parking: Parking available as above
Souvenir Shop(s): Yes
Food & Drinks: Yes

SPECIAL INFORMATION

The North Gloucestershire narrow gauge railway also runs from Toddington Station. Gotherington Halt is now open on the off-peak timetable with access by foot only.

OPERATING INFORMATION

Opening Times: Weekends and Bank Holidays from March to December. Also during selected weekdays – please contact the railway for further details. Trains run from 10.30am to 5.00pm
Steam Working: Most operating days
Prices: Adult Return £11.00
Child Return £6.50
Senior Citizen Return £9.50
Family Return £30.00 (2 Adult + 3 Child)
Under 5's travel free of charge apart from on some Special Event days.

Detailed Directions by Car:
Toddington is 11 miles north east of Cheltenham, 5 miles south of Broadway just off the B4632 (old A46). Exit the M5 at Junction 9 towards Stow-on-the-Wold for the B4632. The Railway is clearly visible from the B4632.

GWILI RAILWAY

Address: Bronwydd Arms Station, Bronwydd Arms, Carmarthen SA33 6HT
Telephone Nº: (01267) 238213
Year Formed: 1975
Location of Line: Near Carmarthen, South Wales
Length of Line: 2½ miles

Nº of Steam Locos: 5
Nº of Other Locos: 6
Nº of Members: 900 shareholders, 450 Society members
Annual Membership Fee: £15.00
Approx Nº of Visitors P.A.: 24,000
Gauge: Standard
Web site: www.gwili-railway.co.uk

GENERAL INFORMATION

Nearest Mainline Station:
Carmarthen (3 miles)
Nearest Bus Station:
Carmarthen (3 miles)
Car Parking: Free parking at Bronwydd Arms except for a few special occasions
Coach Parking:
Free parking at Bronwydd Arms
Souvenir Shop(s): Yes
Food & Drinks: Yes

SPECIAL INFORMATION

Gwili Railway was the first Standard Gauge preserved railway in Wales. There is a riverside picnic area and Miniature railway at Llwyfan Cerrig Station and there is a Signal Box Museum at the Bronwydd Arms.

OPERATING INFO

Opening Times: Bank Holidays from April, some other dates in May then Wednesdays and Sundays in June and July. Daily in August except for Saturdays. Open most weekends in September and December. Also open on certain other dates. Please phone or check the website for further details.
Steam Working: All advertised trains are steam hauled. Trains run from 10.30am to 4.10pm in high season and 11.15am to 3.45pm at other times.
Prices: Adult £6.00
Child £3.00
Family £15.00
(2 adults + up to 2 children)
Senior Citizens £5.00
Note: Discounts are available for groups of 10 or more.

Detailed Directions by Car:
The Railway is three miles North of Carmarthen – signposted off the A484 Carmarthen to Cardigan Road.

HAYLING SEASIDE RAILWAY

Address: Beachlands, Sea Front Road, Hayling Island, Hampshire PO11 0AG
Telephone N°: (02392) 372427
Year Formed: 2001
Location: Beachlands to Eastoke Corner
Length of Line: 1 mile
Web site: www.haylingseasiderailway.co.uk

N° of Steam Locos: Visiting locos only
N° of Other Locos: 4
N° of Members: Approximately 100
Annual Membership Fee: £10.00
Approx N° of Visitors P.A.: 25,000
Gauge: 2 feet

GENERAL INFORMATION

Nearest Mainline Station: Havant
Nearest Bus Station: Beachlands
Car Parking: Spaces are available at both Beachlands and Eastoke Corner.
Coach Parking: Beachlands and Eastoke Corner
Souvenir Shop(s): Yes
Food & Drinks: Available

SPECIAL INFORMATION

The Railway runs along Hayling Island beach front where there are fantastic views across the Solent to the Isle of Wight.

OPERATING INFORMATION

Opening Times: Every Saturday, Sunday and Wednesday throughout the year and daily during the School holidays. Various specials run at different times of the year – please check the web site or phone the Railway for further details. The first train normally departs at 11.00am from Beachlands.
Steam Working: Visiting locos only. Please contact the railway for further information.
Prices: Adult Return £3.50
Child/Senior Citizen Return £2.00
Family Return £7.00 (2 Adult + 2 Child)
Dogs travel free of charge!

Detailed Directions by Car:
Exit the A27 at Havant Roundabout and proceed to Hayling Island and Beachlands Station following the road signs. Parking is available south of the Carousel Amusement Park. Beachlands Station is within the car park.

HIDDEN VALLEY MINIATURE RAILWAY

Address: Hidden Valley Discovery Park, Tredidon St. Thomas, Launceston, Cornwall PL15 8SJ **Telephone Nº**: (01566) 86463 **Year Formed**: 2003 **Location of Line**: Near Launceston **Length of Line**: ¾ mile	**Nº of Steam Locos**: 1 **Nº of Other Locos**: 1 **Approx Nº of Visitors P.A.**: 10,000 **Gauge**: 7¼ inches **Web site**: www.hiddenvalleydiscoverypark.co.uk

GENERAL INFORMATION

Nearest Mainline Station: Liskeard (16 miles)
Nearest Bus Station: Launceston (4 miles)
Car Parking: Available on site
Coach Parking: Available on site
Souvenir Shop(s): Yes
Food & Drinks: Available

SPECIAL INFORMATION

The Railway is situated in Hidden Valley Discovery Park which contains a number of other attractions including a garden railway with over 1,000 feet of track and the 'Crystal Challenges' area.

OPERATING INFORMATION

Opening Times: 2010 dates: 4th to 16th April then from 30th May to 10th September. Also open from 24th to 29th October. Open from 10.00am to 5.00pm with the last admission at 3.00pm each day. Please contact the railway for further details.
Steam Working: Sundays and Wednesdays.
Prices: Adult £6.50
Child £5.50 (Free for ages 4 and under)
Concession £5.00
Family £22.00
Note: The above prices are for entry into the Park which includes the cost of train rides.

Detailed Directions by Car:
Take the A30 from Exeter towards Bodmin and then (shortly after Launceston) take the A395 towards Davidstow and Bude. After about one mile, turn right following the brown tourist signs for 'Hidden Valley'. The railway is located in the Discovery Park approximately ¾ mile along this road.

HOLLYCOMBE STEAM COLLECTION

Address: Hollycombe, Liphook, Hants. GU30 7LP
Telephone Nº: (01428) 724900
Year Formed: 1970
Location of Line: Hollycombe, Liphook
Length of Line: 1¾ miles Narrow gauge, ¼ mile Standard gauge

Nº of Steam Locos: 6
Nº of Other Locos: 2
Nº of Members: 100
Annual Membership Fee: £8.00
Approx Nº of Visitors P.A.: 35,000
Gauge: 2 feet plus Standard & 7¼ inches
Web site: www.hollycombe.co.uk

GENERAL INFORMATION

Nearest Mainline Station: Liphook (1 mile)
Nearest Bus Station: Liphook
Car Parking: Extensive grass area
Coach Parking: Hardstanding
Souvenir Shop(s): Yes
Food & Drinks: Yes – Cafe

SPECIAL INFORMATION

The narrow gauge railway ascends to spectacular views of the Downs and is part of an extensive working steam museum.

OPERATING INFORMATION

Opening Times: 2010 dates: Sundays and Bank Holidays from Easter until the 24th October. Also open Tuesday to Friday in August.
Steam Working: The Standard Gauge steam weekend is held at the start of June 2010 and features a Belgian vertical boiler tank Locomotive. Please contact the railway for further information.
Prices: Adult £11.00
Child £9.00
Senior Citizen £9.00
Family £35.00 (2 adults + 3 children)

Detailed Directions by Car:
Take the A3 to Liphook and follow the brown tourist signs for the railway.

HUNTERS REST MINIATURE RAILWAY

Address: The Hunters Rest Inn, King Lane, Clutton Hill, Bristol BS39 5QL
Telephone Nº: 07962 408463
Year Formed: 1984
Location of Line: Clutton, Near Bath
Length of Line: 500 yards

Nº of Steam Locos: 2
Nº of Other Locos: 2
Nº of Members: –
Approx Nº of Visitors P.A.: Not known
Gauge: 7¼ inches
Web site:
www.huntersrestrailway.webs.com

GENERAL INFORMATION

Nearest Mainline Station: Keynsham (10 miles)
Nearest Bus Station: Bath (11 miles)
Car Parking: Available on site
Coach Parking: Available
Souvenir Shop(s): None
Food & Drinks: Available

SPECIAL INFORMATION

Unusually, this railway is based at an Inn and operations tie in with opening hours.

OPERATING INFORMATION

Opening Times: During the Summer months only (April to October), weather permitting. Open on Sundays from 1.00pm to 4.00pm, Saturdays (in June, July and August) from 5.00pm to 6.30pm and Wednesdays from 6.00pm until dusk.
Steam Working: Please phone the railway for further information.
Prices: Adults £1.00
　　　　　Children £1.00

Detailed Directions by Car:
From All Parts: Take the A37 to Clutton which is located to the south of Bristol between Pensford and Temple Cloud. In Clutton, turn into Station Road then to Clutton Hill. Turn right into King Lane and the Hunters Rest Inn is on the left.

Hythe Ferry Pier Railway

Address: Hythe Ferry Pier, Prospect Place, Hythe SO45 6AU	**N° of Steam Locos**: None
Telephone N°: (023) 8084-0722	**N° of Other Locos**: 2
Year Formed: Installed 1921	**N° of Members**: –
Location of Line: Hythe Pier	**Approx N° of Visitors P.A.**: 500,000
Length of Line: 600 metres	**Gauge**: 2 feet
	Web site: www.hytheferry.co.uk

GENERAL INFORMATION

Nearest Mainline Station: Southampton (2 miles)
Nearest Bus Station: Southampton (2 miles)
Car Parking: Paid parking nearby
Coach Parking: Paid parking nearby
Souvenir Shop(s): Yes – nearby
Food & Drinks: Yes – nearby

SPECIAL INFORMATION

The railway operates along a Victorian Pier and takes passengers to a ferry which operates a regular half-hourly service crossing the harbour from Hythe to Southampton. This is the world's oldest continually working pier train.

OPERATING INFORMATION

Opening Times: The ferry and therefore railway operates daily. The first ferry departs Hythe at 6.10am on weekdays and 7.10am on Saturdays. Sundays and Bank Holidays run from 9.40am to 6.00pm.

Prices: Pier Entrance fee £1.00 (included in the cost of a Ferry ticket)

Note: Ferry fares are an additional charge and vary depending whether they are peak or off-peak.

Detailed Directions by Car:
Hythe Ferry Pier is located by the waterside in Hythe adjacent to the Promenade and the Marina.

Lackham Museum & Woodland Railway

Address: Wiltshire College, Lackham, Lacock SN15 2NY	**Nº of Steam Locos**: 3
	Nº of Other Locos: 3
Telephone Nº: (01225) 753960	**Nº of Members**: –
Year Formed: 2004	**Approx Nº of Visitors P.A.**: 3,000
Location of Line: Wiltshire College	**Gauge**: 7¼ inches
Length of Line: One third of a mile	**Web site**: www.lmandwr.co.uk

GENERAL INFORMATION

Nearest Mainline Station: Chippenham (5 miles)
Nearest Bus Station: Chippenham (5 miles) – take First Bus 234 for Lackham College.
Car Parking: Available on site
Coach Parking: Available
Souvenir Shop(s): None
Food & Drinks: Available on event days only

SPECIAL INFORMATION

This is an railway run by enthusiasts which operates under the alternative name of, 'The Pheasant Line'.

OPERATING INFORMATION

Opening Times: During specific events only. Please check the web site or contact the Museum for further details.
Steam Working: Please contact the Railway for further details – (01225) 753960
Prices: Adults £1.00
Children £1.00

Detailed Directions by Car:
From All Parts: Exit the M4 at Junction 17 and take the A350 past Chippenham to Lacock. The railway runs through the grounds of Wiltshire College and is only open to the public for specific events each year.

LAPPA VALLEY STEAM RAILWAY

Address: St. Newlyn East, Newquay, Cornwall TR8 5LX	**Nº of Steam Locos**: 2
Telephone Nº: (01872) 510317	**Nº of Other Locos**: 2
Year Formed: 1974	**Nº of Members**: –
	Annual Membership Fee: –
Location of Line: Benny Halt to East Wheal Rose, near St. Newlyn East	**Approx Nº of Visitors P.A.**: 50,000
Length of Line: 1 mile	**Gauge**: 15 inches
	Web site: www.lappavalley.co.uk

GENERAL INFORMATION

Nearest Mainline Station: Newquay (5 miles)
Nearest Bus Station: Newquay (5 miles)
Car Parking: Free parking at Benny Halt
Coach Parking: Free parking at Benny Halt
Souvenir Shop(s): Yes
Food & Drinks: Yes

SPECIAL INFORMATION

The railway runs on part of the former Newquay to Chacewater branch line. Site also has a Grade II listed mine building, boating, play areas for children and 2 other miniature train rides.

OPERATING INFORMATION

Opening Times: 2010 dates: Daily from 27th March to 31st October 2010.
Steam Working: 10.30am to 4.30pm or later on operating days
Prices: Adult £9.95 (Off-peak £7.50)
Child £7.95 (Off-peak £5.50)
Family £30.00 (Off-peak £22.00)
(2 adults + 2 children)
Senior Citizen £8.25
(Off-peak £5.80)

Detailed Directions by Car:
The railway is signposted from the A30 at the Summercourt-Mitchell bypass, from the A3075 south of Newquay and the A3058 east of Newquay.

LAUNCESTON STEAM RAILWAY

Address: The Old Gasworks, St. Thomas Road, Launceston, Cornwall PL15 8DA	**Nº of Steam Locos:** 5 (3 working)
	Nº of Other Locos: 2 Diesel, 2 Electric
Telephone Nº: (01566) 775665	**Nº of Members:** Not applicable
Year Formed: Opened in 1983	**Annual Membership Fee:** –
Location of Line: Launceston to Newmills	**Gauge:** 1 foot 11 $\frac{5}{8}$ inches
Length of Line: 2½ miles	**Web site:** www.launcestonsr.co.uk

GENERAL INFORMATION

Nearest Mainline Station: Liskeard (15 miles)
Nearest Bus Station: Launceston (½ mile)
Car Parking: At Station, Newport Industrial Estate, Launceston
Coach Parking: As above
Souvenir Shop(s): Yes – also with a bookshop
Food & Drinks: Yes – Cafe, snacks & drinks

SPECIAL INFORMATION

A new-build steam locomotic will visit the railway during 2010. Please check the web site for details.

OPERATING INFORMATION

Opening Times: 2010 dates: Daily during Easter Week, Whitsun week and during October half-term. Daily from 5th July until the 24th September but closed on Saturdays.
Steam Working: 11.00am to 4.50pm.
Prices: Adult £8.50
Child £5.50
Family £25.00 (2 adults + 4 children)
Senior Citizen £7.00
Group rates are available upon application.

Detailed Directions by Car:
From the East/West: Drive to Launceston via the A30 and look for the brown Steam Engine Tourist signs. Use the L.S.R. car park at the Newport Industrial Estate; From Bude/Holsworthy: Take the A388 to Launceston and follow signs for the town centre. After the river bridge turn left at the traffic lights into Newport Industrial Estate and use the L.S.R. car park.

LITTLEDOWN MINIATURE RAILWAY

Address: Littledown Park, Chaseside, Castle Lane East, Bournemouth, BH7 7DX
Telephone Nº: None
Year Formed: 1924
Location of Line: Littledown Park
Length of Line: Over one third of a mile

Nº of Steam Locos: 15+
Nº of Other Locos: 10+
Nº of Members: 120+
Approx Nº of Visitors P.A.: 4,000
Gauge: 3½ inches, 5 inches & 7¼ inches
Web site: www.littledownrailway.co.uk

GENERAL INFORMATION

Nearest Mainline Station: Bournemouth Central (3½ miles)
Nearest Bus Station: Bournemouth
Car Parking: In Littledown Leisure Centre car park
Coach Parking: As above

SPECIAL INFORMATION

Bournemouth and District Society of Model Engineers operate the railway at Littledown Park.

OPERATING INFORMATION

Opening Times: Most Sundays and Wednesdays throughout the year subject to weather conditions. Trains run from 11.00am to 3.00pm.
Steam Working: Subject to availability. Please contact the railway for further details.
Prices: £1.00 per ride.

Detailed Directions by Car:
The Railway is situated at Littledown Park which is to the North-East of Bournemouth town centre close (and to the South of) the junction of Wessex Way (A338) and Castle Lane (A3060).

LITTLE WESTERN RAILWAY

Address: Trenance Gardens, Trenance Road, Newquay TR7 2HL	**Nº of Steam Locos**: 1 (display only)
	Nº of Other Locos: 1
Telephone Nº: None	**Approx Nº of Visitors P.A.**: Not known
Year Formed: 1965	**Gauge**: 7¼ inches
Location of Line: Newquay, Cornwall	**Web site**: None
Length of Line: 300 yards	

GENERAL INFORMATION

Nearest Mainline Station: Newquay (½ mile)
Nearest Bus Station: Newquay (½ mile)
Car Parking: Available on site
Coach Parking: Available
Souvenir Shop(s): Yes
Food & Drinks: Available

SPECIAL INFORMATION

The railway runs through the floral oasis of Trenance Gardens and close to Newquay Zoo.

OPERATING INFORMATION

Opening Times: Daily during the Summer months.
Steam Working: None at present.
Prices: Adults £1.50 (2 laps of the track)
Children £1.00 (2 laps of the track)

Detailed Directions by Car:
From All Parts: Take the A30 then the A392 to Newquay. At the roundabout turn right to continue along Trevemper Road which becomes the A3058. Turn left into Trenance Road and the gardens are a little way along.

LLANBERIS LAKE RAILWAY

Address: Gilfach Ddu, Llanberis, Gwynedd LL55 4TY	**No of Steam Locos**: 3
Telephone No: (01286) 870549	**No of Other Locos**: 4
Year Formed: 1970	**No of Members**: –
Location of Line: Just off the A4086 Caernarfon to Capel Curig road at Llanberis	**Annual Membership Fee**: –
	Approx No of Visitors P.A.: 80,000
	Gauge: 1 foot 11½ inches
Length of Line: 2½ miles	**Web site**: www.lake-railway.co.uk

GENERAL INFORMATION

Nearest Mainline Station: Bangor (8 miles)
Nearest Bus Station: Caernarfon (6 miles) (there is a bus stop by Llanberis Station)
Car Parking: £3.00 Council car park on site
Coach Parking: Ample free parking on site
Souvenir Shop(s): Yes
Food & Drinks: Yes

SPECIAL INFORMATION

Llanberis Lake Railway runs along part of the trackbed of the Padarn Railway which transported slates for export and closed in 1961. An extension to Llanberis village opened in June 2003.

OPERATING INFORMATION

Opening Times: 2010 dates: Open most days from mid-March to 30th October, daily from 23rd May to 31st August and on certain days during the winter. Please send for a free timetable or check out the railway's web site.
Steam Working: Every operating day. Trains generally run from 11.00am to 4.00pm.
Prices: Adult £7.20
        Child £4.50
        Concessions £6.70
        Family ticket £19.40 (2 Adult + 2 Children)
A range of other family discounts are also available.
Note: The Welsh Slate Museum is situated adjacent to the Railway.

Detailed Directions by Car:
The railway is situated just off the A4086 Caernarfon to Capel Curig road. Follow signs for Padarn Country Park.

LLANGOLLEN RAILWAY

Address: The Station, Abbey Road, Llangollen, Denbighshire LL20 8SN **Telephone Nº**: (01978) 860979 **Year Formed**: 1975 **Location of Line**: Valley of the River Dee from Llangollen to Carrog **Length of Line**: 7½ miles	**Nº of Steam Locos**: 14 **Nº of Other Locos**: 13 **Nº of Members**: 1,400 **Annual Membership Fee**: Adult £18.00; Family £25.00; Junior (under-16) £10.00 **Approx Nº of Visitors P.A.**: 110,000 **Gauge**: Standard

GENERAL INFORMATION

Nearest Mainline Station: Ruabon (6 miles)
Nearest Bus Station: Wrexham (12 miles)
Car Parking: Public car park at Lower Dee Mill off A539 Ruabon road.
Coach Parking: Market Street car park in town centre
Souvenir Shop(s): Yes – at Llangollen Station
Food & Drinks: Yes – at Llangollen, Berwyn, Glyndyfrdwy and Carrog Stations.

SPECIAL INFORMATION

The route originally formed part of the line from Ruabon to Barmouth Junction, closed in 1964. The railway has been rebuilt by volunteers since 1975, reopening to Carrog in 1996.
The ultimate aim is to reopen to Corwen (10 miles).

OPERATING INFORMATION

Opening Times: 2010 dates: Services run daily from 26th March to 17th October. Also on weekends in December, other Santa Specials near Christmas and a number of other dates throughout the year including most days in April and School Holidays.
Steam Working: Phone the Talking timetable number for further details: (01978) 860951
Prices: Adult Day Rover £10.00
Child Day Rover £5.00
Family Day Rover £22.00 (2 adult + 2 child)
Senior Citizen Day Rover £8.00
Note: Tickets for shorter journeys are cheaper.

Web Site: www.llangollen-railway.co.uk

Detailed Directions by Car:
From South & West: Go via the A5 to Llangollen. At the traffic lights turn into Castle Street to the River bridge; From North & East: Take the A483 to A539 junction and then via Trefor to Llangollen River bridge. The Station is adjacent to the River Dee.

LLWYFAN CERRIG MINIATURE RAILWAY

Address: c/o Gwili Railway, Bronwydd Arms SA33 6HT
Telephone Nº: (01267) 230666
Year Formed: 1993
Location of Line: Llwyfan Cerrig Station on the Gwili Railway
Length of Line: 200 yards

Nº of Steam Locos: None
Nº of Other Locos: 2
Nº of Members: 900 shareholders, 450 Society members (Gwili Railway)
Annual Membership Fee: £15.00
Approx Nº of Visitors P.A.: 24,000
Gauge: 7¼ inches
Web site: www.gwili-railway.co.uk

GENERAL INFORMATION

Nearest Mainline Station: Carmarthen (3 miles)
Nearest Bus Station: Carmarthen (3 miles)
Car Parking: Free parking at Bronwydd Arms except for a few special occasions
Coach Parking: Free parking at Bronwydd Arms
Souvenir Shop(s): Yes
Food & Drinks: Yes

SPECIAL INFORMATION

The railway can only be reached via the standard-gauge Gwili Railway line. The cost of rides on the miniature railway are included in the standard gauge railway fares!

OPERATING INFORMATION

Opening Times: Bank Holidays from April, some other dates in May then Wednesdays and Sundays in June and July. Daily in August except for Saturdays. Open most weekends in September and December. Also open on certain other dates. Please phone or check the website for further details.
Steam Working: None
Prices: Adult £6.00
Child £3.00
Family £15.00 (2 adults + up to 2 children)
Senior Citizens £5.00
Note: The above prices are for rides on the standard gauge Gwili Railway. Miniature Railway rides are included in these prices.

Detailed Directions by Car:
Gwili Railway is three miles North of Carmarthen – signposted off the A484 Carmarthen to Cardigan Road. The Llwyfan Cerrig Miniature Railway is only accessible via the Gwili Railway Line.

LYNTON & BARNSTAPLE RAILWAY

Address: Woody Bay Station, Martinhoe Cross, Parracombe, Devon EX31 4RA	**Nº of Steam Locos:** 2
Telephone Nº: (01598) 763487	**Nº of Other Locos:** 1
Year Formed: 1993	**Nº of Members:** 2,200
Location of Line: North Devon	**Annual Membership Fee:** £18.00
Length of Line: One mile	**Approx Nº of Visitors P.A.:** 40,000
	Gauge: 1 foot 11½ inches
	Web site: www.lynton-rail.co.uk

GENERAL INFORMATION

Nearest Mainline Station: Barnstaple
Nearest Bus Station: Barnstaple
Car Parking: Available at Woody Bay Station
Coach Parking: Available by prior arrangement
Souvenir Shop(s): Yes – at Woody Bay Station
Food & Drinks: Available at Woody Bay Station

SPECIAL INFORMATION

Passengers were first carried on a short stretch of this scenic narrow-gauge railway in July 2004. This was the first time the track had been used since the original railway closed in September 1935. The ultimate aim of the Lynton & Barnstaple Railway Trust is to re-open all 19 miles of the line.

OPERATING INFORMATION

Opening Times: Open most days from Easter until the end of October and selected dates in November and December. Please check with the railway for exact dates. Trains run from 10.30am to 4.30pm.
Steam Working: Most trains are steam-hauled except on Mondays and Fridays outside of the school holidays or in the event of breakdown.
Prices: Adult Return £6.00
　　　　　Child Return £3.00 (Under-14s)
　　　　　Senior Citizen Return £4.00
　　　　　Family Ticket £15 (2 Adult + 3 Children)

Detailed Directions by Car:
From All Parts: Woody Bay Station is located alongside the A39 halfway between Lynton and Blackmoor Gate and one mile north-east of the village of Parracombe.

MARGAM PARK RAILWAY

Address: Margam Country Park,
Port Talbot   SA13 2TJ
Telephone Nº: (01639) 881635
Year Formed: 1976
Location of Line: Margam Country Park
Length of Line: 990 yards

Nº of Steam Locos: None
Nº of Other Locos: 1
Nº of Members: –
Approx Nº of Visitors P.A.: 200,000 (to the Park itself)
Gauge: 2 feet
Web site: www.npt.gov.uk/margampark

GENERAL INFO

Nearest Mainline Station:
Port Talbot (3 miles)
Nearest Bus Station:
Port Talbot (3 miles)
Car Parking: Available on site for a £3.50 charge
Coach Parking: Available
Souvenir Shop(s): Yes
Food & Drinks: Available

SPECIAL INFO

Set in 1,000 acres of glorious parkland, Margam Country Park features an 18th Century Orangery, a Tudor-Gothic Victorian Mansion House and a 12th Century Chapter House.

OPERATING INFO

Opening Times: 2010 dates: Daily from 29th March to 5th September. Trains run from 10.00am to 5.00pm.
Steam Working: None
Prices: Adults £1.50
    Children £1.00
    Concessions £1.00
    Family Ticket £4.00
    (2 adults + 2 children)

Detailed Directions by Car:
From All Parts: Exit the M4 at Junction 38 and take the A48 towards Pyle following the brown tourist signs for Margam Country Park. The Park is situated on the left hand side of the road.

MOLD MODEL ENGINEERING SOCIETY

Address: Welsh College of Horticulture, Northop, Mold, Flintshire   CH7 6AA
Phone Nº: (01352) 750492 (Secretary)
Year Formed: 1975
Location of Line: In the grounds of the Welsh College of Horticulture
Length of Line: 1,700 feet

Nº of Steam Locos: 48
Nº of Other Locos: 9
Nº of Members: Approximately 70
Approx Nº of Visitors P.A.: 6,000
Gauge: 3½ inches and 5 inches
Web site: www.moldmes.com

GENERAL INFORMATION

Nearest Mainline Station: Chester (12 miles)
Nearest Bus Station: Mold (3 miles)
Car Parking: Available on site
Coach Parking: Available by prior arrangement
Food & Drinks: None

SPECIAL INFORMATION

The track runs through woodland in the grounds of the Welsh College of Horticulture and is operated by members of the Mold Model Engineering Society.

OPERATING INFORMATION

Opening Times: Sundays throughout the year weather and available staff permitting. Trains run from 11.00am to 4.00pm.
Steam Working: Most Sundays.
Prices: 50p per person per ride although prices may vary during Special events.

Detailed Directions by Car:
The Welsh College of Horticulture is signposted from the crossroads where the A5119 meets the B5126 at traffic lights in the village of Northop. From Mold: Take the A5119 towards Flint and turn left at the traffic lights once in Northop; From the West: Take the A55 towards Chester, turn right onto the A5119 and turn right at the traffic lights in Northop. The College is approximately ¼ mile from the lights. Turn right into the first College entrance and follow the train signs.

MOORS VALLEY RAILWAY

Address: Moors Valley Country Park, Horton Road, Ashley Heath, Nr. Ringwood, Hants. BH24 2ET **Telephone Nº**: (01425) 471415 **Year Formed**: 1985 **Location of Line**: Moors Valley Country Park	**Length of Line**: 1 mile **Nº of Steam Locos**: 15 **Nº of Other Locos**: 2 **Nº of Members**: – **Approx Nº of Visitors P.A.**: 100,000 **Gauge**: 7¼ inches **Web site**: www.moorsvalleyrailway.co.uk

GENERAL INFORMATION

Nearest Mainline Station: Bournemouth (12 miles)
Nearest Bus Station: Ringwood (3 miles)
Car Parking: Parking charges vary throughout the year. Maximum charge £8.00 per day.
Coach Parking: Charges are applied for parking
Souvenir Shop(s): Yes + Model Railway Shop
Food & Drinks: Yes

SPECIAL INFORMATION

The Moors Valley Railway is a complete small Railway with signalling and 2 signal boxes and also 4 tunnels and 2 level crossings.

OPERATING INFORMATION

Opening Times: Weekends throughout the year. Daily from one week before to one week after Easter, Spring Bank Holiday to mid-September, during School half-term holidays and also from Boxing Day to end of School holidays. Also Santa Specials in December and occasional other openings. Phone the Railways for details.
Steam Working: 10.45am to 5.00pm when open.
Prices: Adult Return £3.00;   Adult Single £1.70
  Child Return £2.00;   Child Single £1.20
Special rates are available for parties of 10 or more.

Detailed Directions by Car:
From All Parts: Moors Valley Country Park is situated on Horton Road which is off the A31 Ferndown to Ringwood road near the junction with the A338 to Bournemouth.

MOSELEY INDUSTRIAL NARROW GAUGE TRAMWAY, TOY AND MINING MUSEUM

Address: Tumblydown Farm,
Tolgus Mount, Redruth   TR15 3TA
Telephone Nº: (01209) 211191
Alternative Telephone Nº: 07511 256677
Year Formed: 1969 (formed in the
northwest, relocated to Cornwall in 2000)
Location: ½ mile north of Redruth

Length of Line: 600 yards
Nº of Steam Locos: None
Nº of Other Locos: 15
Nº of Members: 9
Approx Nº of Visitors P.A.: 3,000
Gauge: 2 feet
Web site: www.moseleymuseum.co.uk

GENERAL INFORMATION

Nearest Mainline Station: Redruth (2 miles)
Nearest Bus Station: Redruth (2 miles)
Car Parking: Available on site
Coach Parking: Available by prior arrangement
Souvenir Shop(s): Yes
Food & Drinks: Available by arrangement only

SPECIAL INFORMATION

Moseley Museum is operated by volunteers who
maintain and restore the vehicles and displays.
Other attractions at the museum include collections
of vintage toys and meccano, curios and mining
equipment.

OPERATING INFORMATION

Opening Times: Open throughout the year for
group and individual visits by prior arrangement
only. Please contact the museum for further details.
Steam Working: None at present
Prices: Free of charge but voluntary donations are
gratefully received!

Detailed Directions by Car:
From the A30, turn on to the old Redruth bypass (A3047). Follow the brown tourist signs for Tricky Dickies
Lodge. Tumblydown Farm is on the right about 200 yards past Tricky Dickies.

PAIGNTON & DARTMOUTH STEAM RAILWAY

Address: Queen's Park Station, Torbay Road, Paignton   TQ4 6AF
Telephone Nº: (01803) 555872
Year Formed: 1973
Location of Line: Paignton to Kingswear
Length of Line: 7 miles

Nº of Steam Locos: 6
Nº of Other Locos: 3
Nº of Members: –
Annual Membership Fee: –
Approx Nº of Visitors P.A.: 350,000
Gauge: Standard
Web site: www.dartmouthrailriver.co.uk

GENERAL INFORMATION

Nearest Mainline Station: Paignton (adjacent)
Nearest Bus Station: Paignton (2 minutes walk)
Car Parking: Multi-storey or Mainline Station
Coach Parking: Multi-storey (3 minutes walk)
Souvenir Shop(s): Yes – at Paignton & Kingswear
Food & Drinks: Yes – at Paignton & Kingswear

SPECIAL INFORMATION

A passenger ferry is available from Kingswear Station across to Dartmouth. Combined excursions are also available including train and river trips.

OPERATING INFORMATION

Opening Times: Open daily from May to September (inclusive). Also open on days in April, October and December. Please contact the railway for further information.

Steam Working: Trains run throughout the day from 10.30am to 5.00pm.

Prices: Adult Return   £12.00   (Includes ferry charge)
Child Return   £8.50   (Includes ferry charge)
Family Return   £35.00
2 adults and 2 children
(Includes ferry charge)

Note: Cheaper fares are charged for shorter journeys

Detailed Directions by Car:
From All Parts: Take the M5 to Exeter and then the A380 to Paignton.

Pallot Steam, Motor & General Museum

Address: Rue de Bechet, Trinity, Jersey, JE3 5BE	**Nº of Steam Locos:** 4
Telephone Nº: (01534) 865307	**Nº of Other Locos:** 2
Year Formed: 1990	**Nº of Members:** None
Location of Line: Trinity, Jersey	**Approx Nº of Visitors P.A.:** 12,000
Length of Line: One third of a mile	**Gauge:** Standard and 2 feet
	Web site: www.pallotmuseum.co.uk

GENERAL INFORMATION

Nearest Mainline Station: None
Nearest Bus Station: St. Helier
Car Parking: Available on site
Coach Parking: Available on site
Souvenir Shop(s): Yes
Food & Drinks: Snacks only

SPECIAL INFORMATION

The museum was founded by Lyndon (Don) Pallot who spent his early career as a trainee engineer with the old Jersey Railway.

OPERATING INFORMATION

Opening Times: 2010 dates: Open daily from 1st April to 31st October. Open from 10.00am to 5.00pm. Closed on Sundays.
Steam Working: Every Thursday and also on high-season Tuesdays.
Prices: Adult Museum Admission £5.00
Child Museum Admission £1.50
Under-5s Museum Admission Free of charge
Senior Citizen Museum Admission £4.50
Adult Train Ride £2.00
Child Train Ride £1.20

Detailed Directions by Car:
The museum lies between the A8 and the A9 main roads (Bus Route 5 is easiest) and is signposted off both of these roads.

PENRHYN CASTLE
INDUSTRIAL RAILWAY MUSEUM

Address: Penrhyn Castle, Bangor, LL57 4HN
Telephone N°: (01248) 353084
Year Formed: 1964
Location of Line: Bangor, North Wales
Length of Line: 100 yard demonstration line

N° of Steam Locos: 7
N° of Other Locos: –
Approx N° of Visitors P.A.: 250,000 (to Penrhyn Castle)
Gauge: 2 feet, 4 feet and Standard
Web site: www.nationaltrust.org.uk/penrhyncastle/

GENERAL INFO

Nearest Mainline Station: Bangor (3 miles)
Nearest Bus Station: Bangor (3 miles)
Car Parking: Available on site
Coach Parking: Available
Souvenir Shop(s): Yes
Food & Drinks: Available

SPECIAL INFORMATION

The Museum is situated in Penrhyn Castle, an enormous 19th Century neo-Norman castle which is a National Trust property.

OPERATING INFO

Opening Times: Daily (except for Tuesdays) from 20th Match to 31st October. Open from 12.00pm to 5.00pm.
Steam Working: None – Static displays only.
Prices: Adults £9.00
(Castle Admission)
Children £5.00
(Castle Admission)
Family £22.50
(Castle Admission)
Note: Paid admission to the castle is required to visit the Museum.

Detailed Directions by Car:
From All Parts: Exit the A55 at Junction 11 and take the A5122 towards Bangor. The Castle is clearly visible on the right-hand side of the road.

PERRYGROVE RAILWAY

Address: Perrygrove Railway, Coleford, Gloucestershire GL16 8QB **Telephone Nº**: (01594) 834991 **Year Formed**: 1996 **Location of Line**: ½ mile south of Coleford **Length of Line**: ¾ mile	**Nº of Steam Locos**: 3 **Nº of Other Locos**: 2 **Nº of Members**: 6 **Approx Nº of Visitors P.A.**: Not known **Gauge**: 15 inches **Web site**: www.perrygrove.co.uk

GENERAL INFORMATION

Nearest Mainline Station:
Lydney (for Parkend)
Nearest Bus Station:
Bus stops in Coleford
Car Parking:
Free parking available on site
Coach Parking: Free parking on site
Souvenir Shop(s): Yes
Food & Drinks: Sandwiches & light refreshments are available

SPECIAL INFORMATION

Perrygrove is a unique railway with 4 stations, all with access to private woodland walks. Lots of picnic tables are available in the open and under cover. There is also an indoor village with secret passages, a play area and a new Treetop Adventure playground. The train fare includes admission to all attractions.

OPERATING INFORMATION

Opening Times: Every Saturday, Sunday and Bank Holiday from Easter to Halloween. Daily throughout the local school holidays. Halloween Ghost Trains and Santa Specials also run (pre-booking is essential for these). Please phone for further details. Railway opens at 10.30am with the last train at 4.15pm or 3.45pm depending on the time of year.
Steam Working:
Most services are steam-hauled.
Prices: Adult £5.50 (All-day ticket)
Senior Citizen £5.00
(All-day ticket)
Child (ages 3-16) £4.10
(All-day ticket)

Detailed Directions by Car:
From All Parts: Travel to Coleford, Gloucestershire. Upon reaching the vicinity of Coleford, the Perrygrove Railway is clearly signposted with brown tourist signs from all directions.

PLYM VALLEY RAILWAY

Address: Marsh Mills Station, Coypool Road, Plympton, Plymouth PL7 4NW	**Nº of Steam Locos**: 2
Telephone Nº: (01752) 330881	**Nº of Other Locos**: 4
Year Formed: 1980	**Nº of Members**: 200
Location of Line: Marsh Mills to Lee Moor Crossing, Plympton	**Annual Membership Fee**: £10.00
	Approx Nº of Visitors P.A.: 5,000
Length of Line: ¾ mile	**Gauge**: Standard
	Web site: www.plymrail.co.uk

GENERAL INFORMATION

Nearest Mainline Station: Plymouth (4 miles)
Nearest Bus Station: Plymouth (3 miles)
Car Parking: Available on site
Coach Parking: Available on site
Souvenir Shop(s): Yes
Food & Drinks: Light snacks available

SPECIAL INFORMATION

The ultimate aim of the railway is to rebuild a 1¼ mile section of the ex-Great Western branch line which ran from Tavistock Junction, just outside of Plymouth, through to Launceston. The section to be rebuilt runs from Marsh Mills to Plym Bridge.

OPERATING INFORMATION

Opening Times: Open for static viewing on most Sundays from 11.00am to 5.00pm. Please check the railway's web site or contact the railway directly for information about operating days. Trains run between 1.00pm to 4.00pm on these dates.
Steam Working: Most operating days. Please contact the railway for further details.
Prices: Adult Return £3.00
          Child Return £1.50
Note: There is no charge to visit the station.

Detailed Directions by Car:
Leave the A38 at the Marsh Mills turn-off and take the B3416 towards Plympton. Turn left into Coypool Road just after the McDonalds restaurant. From Plymouth City Centre, take the A374 to Marsh Mills, then as above.

PLYMOUTH MINIATURE STEAM

Address: Goodwin Park,
Pendeen Crescent, Southway, Plymouth
Phone N°: (01752) 201771 (Secretary)
Year Formed: 1970
Location of Line: Goodwin Park Public
Nature Reserve
Length of Line: ½ mile

N° of Steam Locos: 2 + member locos
N° of Other Locos: 2 + member locos
N° of Members: Approximately 100
Approx N° of Visitors P.A.: 2,000
Gauge: 3½ inches, 5 inches & 7¼ inches
Web site: None

GENERAL INFORMATION
Nearest Mainline Station: Plymouth (6 miles)
Nearest Bus Station: Plymouth (6 miles)
Car Parking: Available on site
Coach Parking: None
Food & Drinks: Light refreshments available.

SPECIAL INFORMATION
The railway runs through Goodwin Park, a site
specially developed by members of the Society
which was opened in 1990 and has since been
designated as a Public Nature Reserve.

OPERATING INFORMATION
Opening Times: Open during the 1st and 3rd
Sunday afternoons of each month from April to
October inclusive.
Steam Working: Most operating days.
Prices: 50 per ride.

Detailed Directions by Car:
From the A38 Plymouth Parkway, follow the signs for Tavistock (A386) travelling North until reaching a new
road junction near Plymouth Airport and a Park & Ride site. Turn left at this junction into the Southway Estate
and follow the road for ½ mile past two mini-roundabouts and a set of traffic lights. At the 3rd mini-roundabout
turn left into Pendeen Crescent and about 200 yard on the right is a signpost for the railway. Follow the lane to the
parking area but please note that the bridge has just 6 feet headroom so large vehicles must park outside the track!

PONTYPOOL & BLAENAVON RAILWAY

Address: 13a Broad Street, Blaenavon, Torfaen   NP4 9ND
e-mail: info@pbrly.co.uk
Telephone Nº: (01495) 792263
Year Formed: 1980 (Opened 1983)
Location of Line: Just off the B4248 between Blaenavon and Brynmawr
Length of Line: ¾ mile

Nº of Steam Locos: 9
Nº of Other Locos: 7 + 3 DMUs
Nº of Members: 200
Annual Membership Fee: £12.00
Approx Nº of Visitors P.A.: 5,700
Gauge: Standard
Web site: www.pontypool-and-blaenavon.co.uk

GENERAL INFORMATION

Nearest Mainline Station: Abergavenny (5 miles)
Nearest Bus Station: Blaenavon Town (1½ miles) – regular bus service within ¼ mile (except Sundays)
Car Parking: Free parking for 50 cars on site
Coach Parking: Available on site
Souvenir Shop(s): Yes – at the Station and also a shop at 13 Broad Street, Blaenavon
Food & Drinks: Light refreshments on the train and at the station.

SPECIAL INFORMATION

The railway operates over very steep gradients, is run entirely by volunteers and is the highest standard gauge preserved railway in England and Wales.

OPERATING INFORMATION

Opening Times: 2010 dates: Every weekend and Bank Holiday Monday 5th June to 10th October. Santa Specials and other Special events also run. Please phone the Railway for details or check the web site.
Steam Working: Trains are steam-hauled during Peak days and special steam days. Diesel locos or DMUs may be used on quiet days. Please contact the Railway for further information.
Prices: Adult £4.50
          Child £2.25
          Family £12.00   (2 adults + 3 children)
Fares and conditions may vary for Special Events.

Detailed Directions by Car:
From All Parts: The railway is situated just off the B4248 between Blaenavon and Brynmawr and is well signposted as you approach Blaenavon. Use Junction 25A if using the M4 from the East, or Junction 26 from the West. Head for Pontypool. From the Midlands use the M50, A40 then A465 to Brynmawr. From North & West Wales consider using the 'Heads of the Valleys' A465 to Brynmawr. As you approach the Railway, look out for the Colliery water tower – you can't miss it!

POOLE PARK RAILWAY

Address: Poole Park, Parkstone Road, Poole BH15 1SR
Telephone Nº: 07947 846262
Year Formed: 1949
Location of Line: Poole, Dorset
Length of Line: 1,100 yards

Nº of Steam Locos: 1 (from 1st July 2010)
Nº of Other Locos: 2
Nº of Members: –
Approx Nº of Visitors P.A.: 69,000
Gauge: 10¼ inches
Web site: www.pooleparkrailway.org.uk

GENERAL INFORMATION

Nearest Mainline Station: Poole (½ mile)
Nearest Bus Station: Poole (¼ mile)
Car Parking: Available on site
Coach Parking: Available
Souvenir Shop(s): Yes
Food & Drinks: Available

SPECIAL INFORMATION

The railways circumnavigates a wildfowl lake which is home to wide variety of ducks, geese and swans.

OPERATING INFORMATION

Opening Times: 2010 dates: Daily from 1st March to 5th January then weekends during January and February. Open from 10.00am to 5.00pm.
Steam Working: School Holidays and weekends from 1st July 2010.
Prices: Adults £1.20
Children £1.20

Detailed Directions by Car:
From All Parts: Take the A31 then the A348 to Poole and follow the brown tourist signs for Poole Park.

PORTHMADOG WOODLAND RAILWAY

Address: Tremadog Road, Porthmadog, Gwynedd LL49 9DY	**Nº of Steam Locos**: 3 (at the WHR)
Telephone Nº: (01766) 513402	**Nº of Other Locos**: 18 (at the WHR)
Year Formed: 1961	**Nº of Members**: 1,000
Location of Line: At the Welsh Highland Heritage Railway	**Annual Membership Fee**: £25.00 Adult
	Approx Nº of Visitors P.A.: 25,000
	Gauge: 7¼ inches
Length of Line: 450 yards	**Web site**: www.whr.co.uk

GENERAL INFORMATION

Nearest Mainline Station: Porthmadog (adjacent)
Nearest Bus Station: Services 1 & 3 stop 50 yards away
Car Parking: Free parking at site, plus a public Pay and Display car park within 100 yards
Coach Parking: Adjacent
Souvenir Shop(s): Yes – large range available
Food & Drinks: Yes – excellent home cooking at the Russell Team Room!

SPECIAL INFORMATION

The Porthmadog Woodland Railway is located at the Welsh Highland Heritage Railway. Tickets for the WHHR entitle customers to free rides on the Woodland Railway.

OPERATING INFORMATION

Opening Times: 2010 dates: Daily from 27th March to 31st October inclusive (closed on some Mondays and Fridays during October). Trains run at 10.30am, 11.30am, 1.00pm, 2.00pm, 3.00pm and 4.00pm (the last train runs at 3.00pm during October and November).
Steam Working: 3rd to 11th April; 1st to 3rd May; 29th May to 6th June; Weekends in June and July then daily from 17th July to 5th September; Weekends in September; 23rd to 31st October.
Prices: Adult Day Rover £6.00
Child Day Rover £3.00 (Under-5s free)
Senior Citizen Day Rover £5.00
Family Day Rover £15.00
(2 adults + 2 children)

Detailed Directions by Car:
From Bangor/Caernarfon take the A487 to Porthmadog. From Pwllheli take the A497 to Porthmadog then turn left at the roundabout. From the Midlands take A487 to Portmadog. Once in Porthmadog, follow the brown tourist signs. The line is located right next to Porthmadog Mainline Station, opposite the Queens Hotel.

PURBECK MINIATURE RAILWAY

Address: Purbeck School, Wareham, Dorset BH20 4PF
Contact Telephone Nº: (01929) 556301
Year Formed: 1989
Location of Line: In the grounds of Purbeck School
Length of Line: 245 metres

Nº of Steam Locos: 5
Nº of Other Locos: 4
Nº of Members: 12
Approx Nº of Visitors P.A.: Not known
Gauge: 7¼ inches

GENERAL INFORMATION

Nearest Mainline Station: Wareham (1 mile)
Nearest Bus Station: Wareham (1 mile)
Car Parking: Available on site
Coach Parking: Available
Food & Drinks: Light refreshments available

SPECIAL INFORMATION

The railway usually operates during Car Boot events held at the school and boarding is at Monument Station in the car park. The outward journey runs through the school grounds, across a wildlife pond, through a tunnel and into the main station where visitors can view the engine sheds. A different engine is then coupled to the train for the return journey.

OPERATING INFORMATION

Opening Times: The first Sunday of the month from March to December. Trains run from 9.00am to 1.00pm.
Steam Working: Every operating day.
Prices: £1.00 per ride

Detailed Directions by Car:
Wareham can be approached via the A352 Dorchester road or the A351 Poole to Swanage road. The Purbeck School is situated adjacent to the main roundabout where the A351 and A352 meet.

RHYL MINIATURE RAILWAY

Address: Marine Lake, Wellington Road, Rhyl LL18 1LN	**N° of Steam Locos**: 5
Telephone N°: (01352) 759109	**N° of Other Locos**: 3
Year Formed: 1911	**N° of Members**: Approximately 80
Location of Line: Rhyl	**Annual Membership Fee**: £7.50
Length of Line: 1 mile	**Approx N° of Visitors P.A.**: 9,000
	Gauge: 15 inches
	Web site: www.rhylminiaturerailway.co.uk

GENERAL INFORMATION

Nearest Mainline Station: Rhyl (1 mile)
Nearest Bus Station: Rhyl (1 mile)
Car Parking: Car Park near the Railway
Coach Parking: Available nearby
Souvenir Shop(s): Yes
Food & Drinks: Available

SPECIAL INFORMATION

The trust runs the oldest Miniature Railway in the UK. The principal locomotive and train have been operating there since the 1920's.

OPERATING INFORMATION

Opening Times: Every weekend from Easter until the end of September. Also on Bank Holiday Mondays and daily during the School Summer Holidays. Trains run from 11.00am to 4.00pm.
Steam Working: Every Sunday and also Thursday to Saturday during the School Summer Holidays.
Prices: Adult £2.00
          Child £1.00

Detailed Directions by Car:
From All Parts: The Railway is located behind the west end of Rhyl Promenade.

SAUSMAREZ MANOR MINIATURE RAILWAY

Address: Sausmarez Road, St. Martins, Guernsey, Channel Islands GY4 6SG
Telephone Nº: (01481) 235571
Year Formed: 1985
Location of Line: Guernsey
Length of Line: 400 yards

Nº of Steam Locos: None
Nº of Other Locos: 1
Nº of Members: –
Approx Nº of Visitors P.A.: 4,000
Gauge: 7¼ inches
Web site: www.sausmarezmanor.co.uk

Remus and friends at Sausmarez Manor.

GENERAL INFORMATION

Nearest Mainline Station: Not applicable
Nearest Bus Station: Not applicable
Car Parking: Available on site
Coach Parking: Available
Souvenir Shop(s): Yes
Food & Drinks: Available

SPECIAL INFORMATION

The railway runs through the grounds of Sausmarez Manor, a stately home which dates back to the 13th Century.

OPERATING INFORMATION

Opening Times: Weekends from Easter to October and also daily during the School Holidays. Trains run from 10.00am to 4.00pm.
Steam Working: None
Prices: Adults £2.00
　　　　　Children £1.50
　　　　　Concessions £1.50

Detailed Directions by Car:
Sausmarez Manor is situated 1½ mile to the south of St. Peter's Port, Guernsey.

SNOWDON MOUNTAIN RAILWAY

Address: Llanberis, Caernarfon, Gwynedd, Wales LL55 4TY	**Length of Line:** 4¾ miles
Telephone Nº: 0844 493-8120	**Nº of Steam Locos:** 4
Fax Nº: (01286) 872518	**Nº of Other Locos:** 4
Year Formed: 1894	**Nº of Members:** –
	Approx Nº of Visitors P.A.: 140,000
Location of Line: Llanberis to the summit of Snowdon	**Gauge:** 2 feet 7½ inches
	Web site: www.snowdonrailway.co.uk

GENERAL INFORMATION

Nearest Mainline Station: Bangor (9 miles)
Nearest Bus Station: Caernarfon (7½ miles)
Car Parking: Llanberis Station car park – pay and display. Also other car parks nearby.
Coach Parking: As above but space is very limited
Souvenir Shop(s): Yes
Food & Drinks: Yes

SPECIAL INFORMATION

Britain's only public rack and pinion railway climbs to within 60 feet of the 3,560 feet peak of Snowdon, the highest mountain in England and Wales. The return journey to the summit takes approximately 2½ hours which includes a 30 minute stop at the peak. The new Snowdon Summit Visitor Centre, Hafod Eryri is now open.

OPERATING INFORMATION

Opening Times: 2010 dates: Open daily (weather permitting) from 19th March to 31st October. Trains run every 30 minutes (subject to public demand) from 9.00am until mid/late afternoon. The last departure can be as late as 5.00pm depending on demand. It is advisable to book in advance during school holidays.
Steam Working: Trains may be operated by either steam or diesel depending on engine availability.
Prices: Adult Summit Return £25.00
              Child Summit Return £18.00
Special rates are available for large groups. Please phone 0844 493-8120 for further details.

Detailed Directions by Car:
Llanberis Station is situated on the A4086 Caernarfon to Capel Curig road, 7½ miles from Caernarfon. Convenient access via the main North Wales coast road (A55). Exit at the A55/A5 junction and follow signs to Llanberis via B4366, B4547 and A4086.

SOMERSET & DORSET RAILWAY TRUST MUSEUM

Address: The Railway Station, Washford, Somerset TA23 0PP	**Nº of Steam Locos**: 2
Telephone Nº: (01984) 640869	**Nº of Other Locos**: 1
Year Formed: 1966	**Nº of Members**: –
Location of Line: Washford Station	**Annual Membership Fee**: £18.00 (Adult)
Length of Line: Station sidings only	**Approx Nº of Visitors P.A.**: 3,000
	Gauge: Standard
	Web site: www.sdrt.org.uk

GENERAL INFORMATION

Nearest Mainline Station: Taunton (17 miles)
Nearest Bus Station: Taunton (17 miles)
Car Parking: Available on site
Coach Parking: None
Souvenir Shop(s): Yes
Food & Drinks: None

SPECIAL INFORMATION

The Museum of the Somerset & Dorset Railway Trust contains a mass of exhibits about and memorabilia of this much loved line. This includes a reconstruction of Midford signal box and carriages and wagons including some undergoing restoration.

OPERATING INFORMATION

Opening Times: 2010 dates: 20th, 21st and 25th to 28th March; 2nd to 15th April; daily from 1st May to 3rd October. Also open on 28th and 29th December for a Winter Steam Festival. Open from 10.30am to 5.00pm on these dates. Please check the Museum's web site for further details.
Steam Working: Please contact the Museum or check the web site for further details.
Prices: Adult £2.00
Child £1.00
Family £5.00

Detailed Directions by Car:
The Museum is located at the Railway Station in Washford Village on the A39 Bridgwater to Minehead road.

SOUTH DEVON RAILWAY

Address: Buckfastleigh Station, Buckfastleigh, Devon TQ11 0DZ	**N° of Steam Locos:** 16
Telephone N°: (0845) 345-1427	**N° of Other Locos:** 7
Year Formed: 1969	**N° of Members:** 2,000
Location of Line: Totnes to Buckfastleigh via Staverton	**Annual Membership Fee:** £15.00
	Approx N° of Visitors P.A.: 100,000
Length of Line: 7 miles	**Gauge:** Standard
	Web Site: www.southdevonrailway.co.uk

GENERAL INFORMATION

Nearest Mainline Station: Totnes (¼ mile)
Nearest Bus Station: Totnes (½ mile), Buckfastleigh (Station Road)
Car Parking: Free parking at Buckfastleigh, Council/BR parking at Totnes
Coach Parking: As above
Souvenir Shop(s): Yes – at Buckfastleigh
Food & Drinks: Yes – at Buckfastleigh & on train

SPECIAL INFORMATION

The railway was opened in 1872 as the Totnes, Buckfastleigh & Ashburton Railway.

OPERATING INFORMATION

Opening Times: 2010 dates: Daily from 20th March to 31st October. Santa Specials also run in December. Please contact the railway for further details.
Steam Working: Almost all trains are steam hauled.
Prices: Adult Return £10.00
      Child Return £6.00
      Family Return £29.80
          (2 adults + 2 children)
      Senior Citizen Return £9.50
Note: Extra discounts are available for large groups.

Detailed Directions by Car:
Buckfastleigh is half way between Exeter and Plymouth on the A38 Devon Expressway. Totnes can be reached by taking the A385 from Paignton and Torquay. Brown tourist signs give directions for the railway.

STEAM – MUSEUM OF THE GREAT WESTERN RAILWAY

Address: STEAM – Museum of the Great Western Railway, Kemble Drive, Swindon   SN2 2TA
Telephone Nº: (01793) 466646
Year Formed: 2000

Nº of Steam Locos: 6
Nº of Other Locos: 1
Approx Nº of Visitors P.A.: 100,000
Web site: www.swindon.gov.uk/steam

GENERAL INFORMATION

Nearest Mainline Station: Swindon (10 min. walk)
Nearest Bus Station: Swindon (10 minute walk)
Car Parking: Ample parking space available in the Outlet Centre (charges apply)
Coach Parking: Free parking on site and nearby
Souvenir Shop(s): Yes
Food & Drinks: Yes

SPECIAL INFORMATION

STEAM tells the story of the men and women who built the Great Western Railway.

OPERATING INFORMATION

Opening Times: Open daily all year round from 10.00am to 5.00pm. Closed on 25th, 26th December and 1st January.
Steam Working: During some special events only – please contact the Museum for details.
Prices: Adult Tickets £6.40
  Child Tickets £4.25
  Family Tickets £17.00
  Senior Citizen Tickets £4.25
  Children under 3 are admitted free
Note: Season tickets are also available

Detailed Directions by Car:
Exit the M4 at Junction 16 and follow the brown tourist signs to 'Outlet Centre'. Similarly follow the brown signs from all other major routes.   From the Railway Station: STEAM is a short walk and is accessible through the pedestrian tunnel – entrance by Emlyn Square.

STRAWBERRY LINE MINIATURE RAILWAY

Address: Avon Valley Country Park, Pixash Lane, Keynsham, Bristol, BS31 1TF
Telephone Nº: (0117) 986-0124
Year Formed: 1999
Location of Line:
Length of Line: Two-thirds of a mile

Nº of Steam Locos: 3
Nº of Other Locos: 20
Nº of Members: –
Approx Nº of Visitors P.A.: 100,000
Gauge: 5 inches
Web site: www.strawberryminirail.co.uk

GENERAL INFORMATION

Nearest Mainline Station: Keynsham (2 miles)
Nearest Bus Station: Bath (6 miles)
Car Parking: Available on site
Coach Parking: Available
Souvenir Shop(s): Yes
Food & Drinks: Available

SPECIAL INFORMATION

The Strawberry Line is the only commercial railway in the UK which has a 5 inch gauge.

OPERATING INFORMATION

Opening Times: Daily from Easter until the end of October from 10.00am to 5.00pm.
Steam Working: Frequently – please contact the railway for further details.
Prices: £1.50 per ride

Detailed Directions by Car:
From All Parts: Take the A4 from Bath or Bristol to Keynsham and turn into Pixash Lane following the brown tourist signs for the railway.

SWANAGE RAILWAY

Address: Station House, Railway Station, Swanage, Dorset BH19 1HB
Telephone Nº: (01929) 425800
Year Formed: 1976
Location of Line: Swanage to Norden
Length of Line: 6 miles
Gauge: Standard

Nº of Steam Locos: 5
Nº of Other Locos: 4
Nº of Members: 4,200
Annual Membership Fee: Adult £18.00; Junior/Senior Citizen £12.00; Family 36.00
Approx Nº of Visitors P.A.: 201,448 (exact figures for 2007)
Web site: www.swanagerailway.co.uk

GENERAL INFORMATION

Nearest Mainline Station: Wareham (10 miles)
Nearest Bus Station: Swanage Station (adjacent)
Car Parking: Park & Ride at Norden. Public car parks in Swanage (5 minutes walk)
Coach Parking: Available at Norden
Souvenir Shop(s): Yes – at Swanage Station
Food & Drinks: Yes – buffet available on trains and also Swanage Station Buffet and at Norden.

SPECIAL INFORMATION

The railway runs along part of the route of the old Swanage to Wareham railway, opened in 1885.

OPERATING INFORMATION

Opening Times: Weekends from mid-February and daily from Easter to October. Also open on some other dates throughout the year. Open from 9.30am to 5.00pm.
Steam Working: Most services are steam-hauled. Please check with the Railway for further details.
Prices: Adult Return £9.00
Child Return £7.00
Family Ticket £26.00

Detailed Directions by Car:
Norden Park & Ride Station is situated off the A351 on the approach to Corfe Castle. Swanage Station is situated in the centre of the town, just a few minutes walk from the beach. Take the A351 to reach Swanage.

SWINDON & CRICKLADE RAILWAY

Address: Blunsdon Station, Tadpole Lane, Blunsdon, Swindon, Wilts SN25 2DA	**N° of Steam Locos**: 6
	N° of Other Locos: 7
Phone N°: (01793) 771615	**N° of Members**: 700
Year Formed: 1978	**Annual Membership Fee**: £14.00
Location of Line: Blunsdon to Hayes Knoll	**Approx N° of Visitors P.A.**: 16,000
Length of Line: 1½ miles	**Gauge**: Standard

GENERAL INFORMATION

Nearest Mainline Station: Swindon (5 miles)
Nearest Bus Station: Bus stop at Oakhurst (¾ mile)
Car Parking: Free parking at Blunsdon Station
Coach Parking: Free parking at Blunsdon Station
Souvenir Shop(s): Yes
Food & Drinks: Yes

SPECIAL INFORMATION

The Engine Shed at Hayes Knoll Station is open to the public.

Web site: www.swindon-cricklade-railway.org

OPERATING INFORMATION

Opening Times: The Railway is open every weekend and Bank Holiday throughout the year. Santa Specials run in December and other various special events throughout the year also have Steam train rides. Open 11.00am to 4.00pm.
Steam Working: Every Sunday from Easter until the end of October and certain other dates – please contact the railway for further details.
Prices: Adult £6.00   Child £4.00
　　　　　　Concessions £5.00
　　　　　　Family £18.00
Prices are different for special events.

Detailed Directions by Car:
From the M4: Exit the M4 at Junction 15 and follow the A419. Turn left at Blunsdon Stadium and follow the signs for the Railway: From Cirencester: Follow the A419 to the traffic lights at the top of Blunsdon Hill, then turn right and follow signs for the railway.

TALYLLYN RAILWAY

Address: Wharf Station, Tywyn, Gwynedd, LL36 9EY	**Nº of Steam Locos**: 6
Telephone Nº: (01654) 710472	**Nº of Other Locos**: 4
Year Formed: 1865	**Nº of Members**: 3,500
Location of Line: Tywyn to Nant Gwernol Station	**Annual Membership Fee**: Adult £25.00
	Approx Nº of Visitors P.A.: 50,000
Length of Line: 7¼ miles	**Gauge**: 2 feet 3 inches
	Web site: www.talyllyn.co.uk

GENERAL INFORMATION

Nearest Mainline Station: Tywyn (300 yards)
Nearest Bus Station: Tywyn (300 yards)
Car Parking: 100 yards away
Coach Parking: Free parking (100 yards)
Souvenir Shop(s): Yes
Food & Drinks: Yes

SPECIAL INFORMATION

Talyllyn Railway was the first preserved railway in the world – saved from closure in 1951. The railway was originally opened in 1866 to carry slate from Bryn Eglwys Quarry to Tywyn. Among the railway's attractions are a Narrow Gauge Railway Museum at the Tywyn Wharf terminus.

OPERATING INFORMATION

Opening Times: 2010 dates: Daily from 28th March to 31st October. Generally open from 10.00am to 5.00pm (later during the summer). Also open for Santa/New Year Specials on some dates in November, December and January.
Steam Working: All services are steam-hauled.
Prices: Adult Return £12.50 (Day Rover ticket) Children (ages 5-15) pay £3.00 if travelling with an adult. Otherwise, they pay half adult fare. Children under the age of 5 travel free of charge.
The fares shown above are for a full round trip. Tickets to intermediate stations are cheaper.

Detailed Directions by Car:
From the North: Take the A493 from Dolgellau into Tywyn; From the South: Take the A493 from Machynlleth to Tywyn.

TANAT VALLEY LIGHT RAILWAY

Address: Nant Mawr Visitor Centre, Nant Mayr Quarry, Lower Bowl, Nant Mawr, Oswestry SY10 9HW
Telephone Nº: (01691) 610234
Year Formed: 2004
Location of Line: Nant Mawr Quarry
Length of Line: One third of a mile

Nº of Steam Locos: None
Nº of Other Locos: 3
Nº of Members: 100+
Annual Membership Fee: £10.00
Approx Nº of Visitors P.A.: 5,000+
Gauge: Standard
Web site: www.tvlr.co.uk

GENERAL INFORMATION

Nearest Mainline Station: Gobowen (5 miles)
Nearest Bus Station: Oswestry (5 miles)
Car Parking: Available on site
Coach Parking: None
Souvenir Shop(s): Yes
Food & Drinks: None

SPECIAL INFORMATION

Other attractions at the railway include Woodland Walks, a picnic area and a Nature Trail.

OPERATING INFORMATION

Opening Times: Most weekends from 10.00am to 4.00pm and at other times by prior arrangement. Please contact the railway for further information.
Steam Working: None at present. Static displays only.
Prices: No charge although donations are gratefully received. Footplate rides may be available on occasional dates in 2010. Please contact the railway for further information.

Detailed Directions by Car:
From All Parts: Take the A5 to the Oswestry bypass then follow the A483 signposted for Welshpool. At the Llynclys Crossroads, turn right onto the A495 and, after about 2 miles, turn right at Blodwell Bank then take the first left and an immediate right turn for the railway.

TEIFI VALLEY RAILWAY

Address: Henllan Station, Henllan, near Newcastle Emlyn, Carmarthenshire	**Nº of Steam Locos**: 2
Telephone Nº: (01559) 371077	**Nº of Other Locos**: 3
Year Formed: 1978	**Nº of Members**: Approximately 150
Location of Line: Between Cardigan and Carmarthen off the A484	**Annual Membership Fee**: £12.00
Length of Line: 2 miles	**Approx Nº of Visitors P.A.**: 15,000
	Gauge: 2 feet
	Web site: www.teifivalleyrailway.com

GENERAL INFORMATION

Nearest Mainline Station: Carmarthen (10 miles)
Nearest Bus Station: Carmarthen (10 miles)
Car Parking: Spaces for 70 cars available.
Coach Parking: Spaces for 4 coaches available.
Souvenir Shop(s): Yes
Food & Drinks: Yes (snacks only)

SPECIAL INFORMATION

The Railway was formerly part of the G.W.R. but now runs on a Narrow Gauge using Quarry Engines.

OPERATING INFORMATION

Opening Times: 2010 dates: Open daily from 2nd April until the end of September (closed some Fridays). Open on weekends in October and daily from 25th to 30th October. Also open on some days in December for 'Santa Specials'. Trains run from 11.00am – 4.30pm.
Steam Working: Most operating days – please phone the Railway for further details.
Prices: Adult £6.00
Child £4.00
Senior Citizen £5.50
A 10% discount is available for parties of 10 or more.

Detailed Directions by Car:
From All Parts: The Railway is situated in the Village of Henllan between the A484 and the A475 (on the B4334) about 4 miles east of Newcastle Emlyn.

TODDINGTON NARROW GAUGE RAILWAY

Address: The Station, Toddington, Cheltenham, Gloucestershire GL54 5DT	**N° of Steam Locos**: 3
Telephone N°: (01242) 621405	**N° of Other Locos**: 5
Year Formed: 1985	**N° of Members**: Approximately 35
Location of Line: 5 miles south of Broadway, Worcestershire, near the A46	**Annual Membership Fee**: £6.00
Length of Line: ½ mile	**Approx N° of Visitors P.A.**: 2,000
	Gauge: 2 feet
	Web site: www.toddington-narrow-gauge.co.uk

GENERAL INFORMATION

Nearest Mainline Station: Cheltenham Spa or Ashchurch
Nearest Bus Station: Cheltenham
Car Parking: Parking available at Toddington, Winchcombe & Cheltenham Racecourse Stations
Coach Parking: Parking available as above
Souvenir Shop(s): None
Food & Drinks: None at the TNGR itself but available at the adjacent GWSR site.

SPECIAL INFORMATION

The railway boasts the only German-built World War One Henschel locomotive in this country.

OPERATING INFORMATION

Opening Times: 2010 dates: 4th & 5th April; 2nd, 3rd, 29th, 30th & 31st May; 5th, 6th, 13th, 20th & 27th June; 4th, 11th, 18th & 25th July; 1st, 8th, 15th, 22nd, 29th & 30th August; 25th & 26th September (Thomas the Tank Engine); 24th & 31st October; 29th & 30th December. Trains usually run from every 35 minutes from around noon.
Steam Working: Most operating days
Prices: Adults £2.00
　　　　　Children £1.00 (Under-5s ride free)

Detailed Directions by Car:
Toddington is 11 miles north east of Cheltenham, 5 miles south of Broadway just off the B4632 (old A46). Exit the M5 at Junction 9 towards Stow-on-the-Wold for the B4632. The Railway is clearly visible from the B4632.

VALE OF RHEIDOL RAILWAY

Address: The Locomotive Shed, Park Avenue, Aberystwyth, Dyfed SY23 1PG **Telephone Nº**: (01970) 625819 **Year Formed**: 1902 **Location of Line**: Aberystwyth to Devil's Bridge **Length of Line**: 11¾ miles	**Nº of Steam Locos**: 3 **Nº of Other Locos**: 1 **Nº of Members**: None **Annual Membership Fee**: – **Approx Nº of Visitors P.A.**: 38,000 **Gauge**: 1 foot 11¾ inches **Web site**: www.rheidolrailway.co.uk

GENERAL INFORMATION

Nearest Mainline Station: Aberystwyth (adjacent)
Nearest Bus Station: Aberystwyth (adjacent)
Car Parking: Available on site
Coach Parking: Parking available 400 yards away
Souvenir Shop(s): Yes
Food & Drinks: Yes

SPECIAL INFORMATION

The journey between the stations take one hour in each direction. At Devil's Bridge there is a cafe, toilets, a picnic area and the famous Mynach Falls. The line climbs over 600 feet in 11¾ miles.

OPERATING INFORMATION

Opening Times: 2010 dates: Open almost every day from 1st April to 30th October with some exceptions. Please phone the railway for further information.
Steam Working: All trains are steam-hauled. Trains run from 10.30am to 4.00pm on most days.
Prices: Adult Return £14.00
Child Return – First 2 children per adult pay £3.50 each. Further children pay £7.00 each

---

Detailed Directions by Car:
From the North take A487 into Aberystwyth. From the East take A470 and A44 to Aberystwyth. From the South take A487 or A485 to Aberystwyth. The Station is joined on to the Mainline Station in Alexandra Road.

WELSH HIGHLAND RAILWAY

Postal Address: Ffestiniog Railway, Harbour Station, Porthmadog LL49 9NF	**Nº of Steam Locos:** 7 (4 working)
Telephone Nº: (01766) 516000	**Nº of Other Locos:** 3
Year Formed: 1997	**Nº of Members:** 2,300
Location: Caernarfon to Pont Croesor (extension opening during 2010)	**Annual Membership Fee:** £25.00
Length of Line: 19 miles	**Approx Nº of Visitors P.A.:** 50,000
	Gauge: 1 foot 11½ inches
	Web site: www.festrail.co.uk

GENERAL INFORMATION

Nearest Mainline Station: Bangor (7 miles) (Bus service Nº 5 runs to Caernarfon)
Nearest Bus Station: Caernarfon
Car Parking: Parking available at Caernarfon
Coach Parking: At Victoria Docks (¼ mile)
Souvenir Shop(s): Yes
Food & Drinks: Light refreshments on most trains

SPECIAL INFORMATION

The Railway is being reconstructed between Caernarfon and Porthmadog along the track bed of the original Welsh Highland Railway. An extension through the spectacular scenery of the Aberglaslyn Pass opened in 2009 and a further extension to Pont Croesor is scheduled to open in May 2010 with completion to Porthmadog in 2011.

OPERATING INFORMATION

Opening Times: Regular services run from Easter to the end of October. There is also a limited service in the Winter. Train times vary depending on the date. Please contact the railway for further details.
Steam Working: Most trains are steam-hauled.
Prices: Adult £28.00 (All-day Rover ticket)
One child travels free with each adult, additional children travel for half the fare.
Concessionary prices are available for Senior Citizens and groups of 20 or more and cheaper fares are available for single rides and shorter journeys.

Detailed Directions by Car:
Take either the A487(T), the A4085 or the A4086 to Caernarfon then follow the brown tourist signs for the Railway which is situated in St. Helens Road next to the Castle.

WELSH HIGHLAND HERITAGE RAILWAY

Address: Tremadog Road, Porthmadog, Gwynedd LL49 9DY	**N° of Steam Locos**: 3
Telephone N°: (01766) 513402	**N° of Other Locos**: 18
Year Formed: 1961	**N° of Members**: 1,000
Location of Line: Opposite Porthmadog Mainline Station	**Annual Membership Fee**: £25.00 Adult
	Approx N° of Visitors P.A.: 25,000
Length of Line: 1½ mile round trip	**Gauge**: 1 foot 11½ inches
	Web site: www.whr.co.uk

GENERAL INFORMATION

Nearest Mainline Station: Porthmadog (adjacent)
Nearest Bus Station: Services 1 & 3 stop 50 yards away
Car Parking: Free parking at site, plus a public Pay and Display car park within 100 yards
Coach Parking: Adjacent
Souvenir Shop(s): Yes – large range available
Food & Drinks: Yes – excellent home cooking at the Russell Team Room!

SPECIAL INFORMATION

The Welsh Highland Railway is a family-orientated attraction based around a Railway Heritage Centre and includes a guided, hands-on tour of the sheds. A ¾ mile extension to Traeth Mawr is now open.

OPERATING INFORMATION

Opening Times: 2010 dates: Daily from 27th March to 31st October inclusive (closed on some Mondays and Fridays during October). Trains run at 10.30am, 11.30am, 1.00pm, 2.00pm, 3.00pm and 4.00pm (the last train runs at 3.00pm during October and November).
Steam Working: 3rd to 11th April; 1st to 3rd May; 29th May to 6th June; Weekends in June and July then daily from 17th July to 5th September; Weekends in September; 23rd to 31st October.
Prices: Adult Day Rover £6.00
Child Day Rover £3.00 (Under-5s free)
Senior Citizen Day Rover £5.00
Family Day Rover £15.00
(2 adults + 2 children)

Detailed Directions by Car:
From Bangor/Caernarfon take the A487 to Porthmadog. From Pwllheli take the A497 to Porthmadog then turn left at the roundabout. From the Midlands take A487 to Portmadog. Once in Porthmadog, follow the brown tourist signs. The line is located right next to Porthmadog Mainline Station, opposite the Queens Hotel.

WELSHPOOL & LLANFAIR LIGHT RAILWAY

Address: The Station, Llanfair Caereinion, Powys SY21 0SF	**Nº of Steam Locos:** 9
Telephone Nº: (01938) 810441	**Nº of Other Locos:** 5
Year Formed: 1959	**Nº of Members:** 1,900
Location of Line: Welshpool to Llanfair Caereinion, Mid Wales	**Annual Membership Fee:** £22.50
	Approx Nº of Visitors P.A.: 26,000
	Gauge: 2 feet 6 inches
Length of Line: 8 miles	**Web site:** www.wllr.org.uk

GENERAL INFORMATION

Nearest Mainline Station: Welshpool (1 mile)
Nearest Bus Station: Welshpool (1 mile)
Car Parking: Free parking at Welshpool and Llanfair Caereinion
Coach Parking: As above
Souvenir Shop(s): Yes – at both ends of line
Food & Drinks: Yes – at Llanfair only

SPECIAL INFORMATION

The railway has the steepest gradient of any British railway, reaching a summit of 603 feet.

OPERATING INFORMATION

Opening Times: 2010 dates: Easter, Bank Holidays and weekends from 3rd April to 31st October. Daily from 17th July to 5th September. Most other days in June and July plus dates in September, October and December. Generally open from 9.30am to 5.00pm.
Steam Working: All trains are steam-hauled
Prices: Adult £11.80
    Senior Citizens £10.80
Children under the age of 3 travel free of charge. The first child aged 3-15 per adult travels for £1.00. All other children are charged half-price – £5.90

Detailed Directions by Car:
Both stations are situated alongside the A458 Shrewsbury to Dolgellau road and are clearly signposted

WEST SOMERSET RAILWAY

Address: The Railway Station, Minehead, Somerset TA24 5BG **Telephone Nº**: (01643) 704996 (enquiries) **Year Formed**: 1976 **Location of Line**: Bishops Lydeard (near Taunton) to Minehead **Length of Line**: 19¾ miles	**Nº of Steam Locos**: 7 **Nº of Other Locos**: 12 **Nº of Members**: 5,000 **Annual Membership Fee**: £17.00 **Approx Nº of Visitors P.A.**: 220,000 **Gauge**: Standard **Web site**: www.west-somerset-railway.co.uk

GENERAL INFORMATION

Nearest Mainline Station: Taunton (4 miles)
Nearest Bus Station: Taunton (4½ miles) – Services 18 & 28 run to Bishops Lydeard.
Car Parking: Free parking at Bishops Lydeard; Council car parking at Minehead and Watchet
Coach Parking: As above
Souvenir Shop(s): Yes – at Minehead, Bishops Lydeard and Washford
Food & Drinks: Yes – At some stations. Buffet and Dining cars on all trains.

SPECIAL INFORMATION

Britain's longest Standard gauge Heritage railway runs through the Quantock Hills and along the Bristol Channel Coast. The line passes through no fewer than ten Stations with museums at Washford and Blue Anchor and a turntable at Minehead.

OPERATING INFORMATION

Opening Times: 2010 dates: Various dates from February to December including daily from 27th April to 3rd October. Open 9.30am to 5.30pm. Please contact the railway for more detailed dates.
Steam Working: All operating days except during Diesel Galas.
Prices: Adult Day Rover £14.80
Child Day Rover £7.40
Family Rover £42.00 (2 adult + 4 child)
Senior Citizen Day Rover £13.40

Detailed Directions by Car:
Exit the M5 at Taunton (Junction 25) and follow signs for A358 to Williton and then the A39 for Minehead. In Minehead, brown tourist signs give directions to the railway.

WESTON MINIATURE RAILWAY

Address: Marine Parade, Weston-super-Mare, Somerset
Telephone Nº: (01934) 643510
Year Formed: 1981
Location of Line: Marine Parade
Length of Line: 900 yards

Nº of Steam Locos: 1
Nº of Other Locos: 3
Approx Nº of Visitors P.A.: 20,000
Gauge: 7¼ inches
Web site: www.westonminiaturerailway.co.uk

GENERAL INFORMATION

Nearest Mainline Station: Weston-super-Mare
Nearest Bus Station: Weston-super-Mare
Car Parking: Available nearby on the seafront
Coach Parking: Available on the seafront
Souvenir Shop(s): Yes
Food & Drinks: Available

SPECIAL INFORMATION

This is a popular tourist railway running along the Weston-super-Mare seafront.

OPERATING INFORMATION

Opening Times: Daily from Spring Bank Holiday until September. Also open at weekends from February to October.
Steam Working: Some Sundays.
Prices: Adult £1.50
          Child £1.50

Detailed Directions by Car:
From All Parts: The Railway is situated at the Southern end of the seafront in Weston-super-Mare. Follow the brown tourist signs

---

WESTON PARK RAILWAY

Address: Weston Park, Weston-under-Lizard, Shifnal, Shropshire TF11 8LE
Telephone Nº: (05601) 132334 (Railway) or (01952) 852100 (Weston Park)
Year Formed: 1980
Location of Line: Weston Park

Length of Line: Approximately 1¼ miles
Nº of Steam Locos: Variable
Nº of Other Locos: Variable
Approx Nº of Visitors P.A.: 19,500
Gauge: 7¼ inches
Web site: www.weston-park.com

GENERAL INFORMATION

Nearest Mainline Station: Shifnal (6 miles)
Nearest Bus Station: –
Car Parking: Available on site
Coach Parking: Available on site
Souvenir Shop(s): –
Food & Drinks: Available

SPECIAL INFORMATION

The railway operates in the grounds of Weston Park, a stately home with a large park and gardens designed by 'Capability' Brown. Weston Park also has a number of other attractions for all the family.

OPERATING INFORMATION

Opening Times: 2010 dates: Daily from 29th May to 5th September. Please contact Weston Park for further details about weekend opening.
Steam Working: Please contact the railway for further details: info@westonrail.co.uk
Prices: Adults £2.00
Children £1.50
Note: Prices shown above are for train fares only. An admission charge is made for entry into the park, gardens and stately home. This admission fee is required for use of the railway. Please contact Weston Park for admission price information.

Detailed Directions by Car:
From All Parts: Weston Park is situated by the side of the A5 in Weston-under-Lizard, Shropshire, just 3 miles from the M54 (exit at Junction 3 and take the A41 northwards) and 8 miles West of the M6 (exit at Junction 12).

WOODLAND RAILWAY

Address: Brokerswood Country Park, Westbury BA13 4EH	**N° of Steam Locos:** None
Telephone N°: (01373) 822238	**N° of Other Locos:** 1
Year Formed: –	**N° of Members:** –
Location of Line: West Wiltshire	**Approx N° of Visitors P.A.:** 60,000
Length of Line: Two-thirds of a mile	**Gauge:** 10¼ inches
	Web site: www.brokerswoodcountrypark.co.uk

GENERAL INFORMATION

Nearest Mainline Station: Westbury (2 miles)
Nearest Bus Station: Bath (12 miles)
Car Parking: Available on site
Coach Parking: Available
Souvenir Shop(s): Yes
Food & Drinks: Available

SPECIAL INFORMATION

The railway runs through the award-winning Brokerswood Country Park, a precious 80 acre fragment of the ancient forest of Selwood.

OPERATING INFORMATION

Opening Times: Weekends and daily during the School Holidays from Easter until the end of October. Open from 10.00am to 5.00pm.
Steam Working: None
Prices: Adult Return £1.00
Child Return £1.00

Detailed Directions by Car:
From All Parts: Exit the M4 at Junction 18 and take the A46 to Bath then the A36 to Beckington services. Turn left onto the A361 towards Southwick then follow the brown tourist signs to Brokerswood Country Park.

YEOVIL RAILWAY CENTRE

Address: Yeovil Junction Station, Stoford, Yeovil BA22 9UU	**N° of Steam Locos**: 1
	N° of Other Locos: 3
Telephone N°: (01935) 410420	**N° of Members**: 300
Year Formed: 1993	**Annual Membership Fee**: £12.50
Location of Line: Yeovil Junction	**Approx N° of Visitors P.A.**: 5,000
Length of Line: ¼ mile	**Web site**:
Gauge: Standard	www.yeovilrailway.freeservers.com

GENERAL INFORMATION

Nearest Mainline Station: Yeovil Junction (adjacent)
Nearest Bus Station: A regular bus service runs from Yeovil Bus Station (2 miles)
Car Parking: Available on site
Coach Parking: Available nearby
Souvenir Shop(s): Yes
Food & Drinks: Available

SPECIAL INFORMATION

The Visitor Centre is located in a GWR Transfer Shed which was built in 1864.
The centre also runs Driver Experience days.

OPERATING INFORMATION

Opening Times: Open regularly for Steam Train days, Mainline steam visits and other special events from March to October. Also open for Santa Specials in December and for static viewing every Sunday morning from 10.00am until noon. Please contact the Centre for further details of event days.
Steam Working: The Yeovil 150 Celebration is on the 17th & 18th July 2010. Please contact the Centre for further details.
Prices: Adult £5.00
         Child £2.50 (Ages 5 to 15)
Note: Prices shown above are for Steam Working days.

Detailed Directions by Car:
The Centre is part of Yeovil Junction Station which is served by South West Trains. By road simply follow the signs to Yeovil Junction Station from Yeovil town centre or from the A37 Dorchester to Yeovil road. The entrance to Yeovil Railway Centre is through the low bridge, half way up the Yeovil Junction Station approach road.

GREAT ORME TRAMWAY

Address: Victoria Station, Church Walks, Llandudno LL30 2NB	**Nº of Steam Locos**: None
Telephone Nº: (01492) 879306	**Nº of Other Locos**: 4 tram units
Year Formed: 1902	**Approx Nº of Visitors P.A.**: 200,000
Location of Line: North Walk, Llandudno	**Gauge**: 3 feet 6 inches
Length of Line: Approximately 1 mile	**Web site**: www.greatormetramway.co.uk

GENERAL INFORMATION

Nearest Mainline Station: Llandudno (½ mile)
Nearest Bus Station: Llandudno (½ mile)
Car Parking: Available at the Summit only
Coach Parking: Available at the Summit only
Souvenir Shop(s): Yes
Food & Drinks: Available

SPECIAL INFORMATION

The Great Orme Tramway still uses the original tramcars and is the only cable-hauled tramway still operating on Britain's public roads. The track itself climbs 679 feet to the Summit Station providing panoramic views of Llandudno Bay.

OPERATING INFORMATION

Opening Times: Daily from late March until late October with trams running from 10.00am to 6.00pm (until 5.00pm in March and October).
Steam Working: None
Prices: Adult Return £5.60
  Child Return £3.80
Note: Discounted prices for families and larger groups are also available.

Detailed Directions by Car:
From All Parts: Take the A55 Expressway to the Llandudno Junction turn-off just next to the Conwy Road Tunnel and follow the A546 through Deganwy into Llandudno. Upon reaching the seafront, turn left into North Parade adjacent to the pier then left again into Church Walks. Victoria Station is about 300 yards on the right.

SEATON TRAMWAY

Address: Riverside Depot, Harbour Road, Seaton EX12 2NQ	**Nº of Steam Locos:** None
	Nº of Other Locos: 14 trams
Telephone Nº: (01297) 20375	**Approx Nº of Visitors P.A.:** 100,000+
Year Formed: 1970	**Gauge:** 2 feet 9 inches
Location of Line: Seaton to Colyton, East Devon	**Web site:** www.tram.co.uk
Length of Line: 3 miles	

GENERAL INFO

Nearest Mainline Station: Axminster (6½ miles)
Nearest Bus Station: Seaton
Car Parking: Available on site
Coach Parking: Available on site
Souvenir Shop(s): Yes
Food & Drinks: Available at the Tramstop Restaurant

SPECIAL INFO

The Seaton Tramway follows a section of the former Southern Railway branch line which runs through East Devon's Axe Valley from the coastal resort of Seaton to the medieval town of Colyton. The track itself passes along the estuary of the River Axe through two nature reserves and offers excellent views of wading birds and other wildlife.

OPERATING INFO

Opening Times: 2010 dates: Trams run daily from 27th March until 31st October and weekends from 6th November to 18th December. Trams run from 10.00am on most operating days.
Steam Working: Not applicable
Prices: Adult Return £8.35
Child Return £5.85
Concessions Return £7.50
Note: Different fares apply for Loyalty Card holders and single journeys and special family rates are also available.

Detailed Directions by Car:
From All Parts: Seaton Tramway is situated at the mouth of the River Axe at the side of the B3172 which can be accessed via the A358 or A3052 roads.